This is our Promised Land

Olympia Rizidis

First published 2012

National Library of Australia Cataloguing-in-Publication entry:

Author:	Rizidis, Olympia.
Title:	This is our promised land / Olympia Rizidis.
ISBN:	9781921920318 (pbk.)
	9781921920349 (ebook)
Subjects:	Rizidis, Olympia--Family.
	Families--Greece--Biography.
	Women--Biography.
	Greece--Genealogy.
Dewey Number:	306.8509495

Typeset in Perpetua 13pt.

Cover Design by Boolarong Press

Published by Boolarong Press, Salisbury, Brisbane, Australia.

Printed and bound by Watson Ferguson & Company, Salisbury, Brisbane, Australia.

Acknowledgements

My first acknowledgement is for my husband Tony Pearce and his great patience and love. Without his encouragement and support this book would never have been written.

To my late parents who suffered many hardships but always tried to do the best they could for their family and friends.

To my children - my son Vasilios and his wife Helen for reading the manuscript and their encouragements, and to my daughter Maria for her loving support throughout the years.

My brothers Hercules and Eleftherios. In loving memory of both my brothers as both of them have gone to be with the Lord Jesus but their love will always live in my heart.

My loving sister Anastasia (Tasoula) for her support.

My friends Betty and Carle for their wonderful assistance in helping me with my English expression.

And to the following relations and friends who have guided my life and who have provided me with much background for my story: *Papou*

Zacharia, *Thea* Sapfo and *Theo* George, *Thea* Anna and *Theo* George, *Giagia* Malamati, *Thea* Mersina, *Theo* Kuriakos and *Thea* Eleftheria, *Theo* Pluto and *Thea* Fretheriki, *Thea* Chrissy and *Theo* Thomas, *Thea* Taso and *Theo* Thanasos, *Thea* Chrissy and *Theo* Stellios, *Thea* Anastasia and *Theo* Manolis, Elizabeth and Vic, Anna and John Paioff, Theo and Helen Emmanouilidis, Despina and Thanasis Rovolidis, Theodore Diamandopoulos, Soule Pirzas, Iona Papajesik, Rev Carol Hebron.

To Susanna De Vries a big thank you for encouraging me to approach Boolarong publishers.

Thank you Dan Kelly and your team at Boolarong Publishers, for all your help so that this book has been published at last.

And a big thank you to Colin and Deidrie from Canterbury Tours who organized our trip to find my father's house in Kouvouklia (Gorukle) in Turkey in October 2008.

I am grateful to all my family and friends for their support, encouragement that has helped me to keep writing this story. I am blessed by each person who has crossed my path.

This is my story, my family's history. It is my journey, it is my recollection and the fond memories I still have of those years growing up and being blessed by my *Papou*, *Giagia*, *Mama*, *Baba*, Hercules, Eleutherios, Anastasia, my loving sisters in law Aspa and Anna, my brother in law Kon, nieces and nephews and all my precious *Theas* and *Theos, cousins* and friends. Thank you all for enriching my life.

Olympia Rizidis

O Christos Nika Ta Pannda (Christ Conquers All.)

Contents

Preface

My life has been a wonderful journey with my family and friends. My family's roots, traditions and memories bind us together. I feel privileged as all of these people have touched and encouraged me in one way or another. Growing up and hearing the stories of their faith, hope and love of God have guided my life's journey and made me into who I am.

Every person who crossed my path is a gift; a blessing of God's great love. Their lives and blessings were my gifts. Listening to their stories fascinated me. Many of them had survived wars, persecutions and refugee camps. They had been prisoners of war and were uprooted from their homes and lands.

These precious memories of my loved ones are what I am today. I belong and I am part of them. Their stories are my heritage, my roots and my life. Their stories have all enriched me in my life's journey, a life full of blessings of love and caring. So I begin my story with my *Baba* (father), whose Asia Minor Greek name was Giannko Rizougloudzins. His Greek name was Gianni Rizidis.

My *Baba* was born in the village of Kouvoukleia near the city of Prousa in Turkey. The new Turkish name for the village is Gorukle. The two-storey house was built with rocks, stone and handmade mud bricks; the family lived upstairs while the animals they had were housed downstairs. They had a bullock to haul their cart and plough their fields, a horse or mule for transport and sheep and goats for milk and meat. Chickens provided eggs and meat, while dogs were used to guard the house, or for hunting, and cats were kept to keep the barns free from rats.

The villagers' lives were peaceful as they went about their daily work planting and harvesting their various crops. Men worked in the fields while women looked after their homes, children and the old parents, as they all lived in the one house. They married, had children and lived a serene life of looking after their family until they died. Many did not even venture out of their village unless it was to visit Prousa (now Bursa), the closest city. They worked every day in the fields, producing their vegetables, grapes, wheat, and fruit such as figs, apples, pomegranate and mulberries. The village had silk workshops, shoemakers, tailors, blacksmiths, carpenters and builders.

The area was on the Silk Road. Silk was one of the area's main industries. My *Baba's* maternal and paternal grandparents had a thriving silk industry in Kouvoukleia, with the family taking their handicrafts to Prousa, Constantinople or Smyrna. They lived above their silk workshops. The supply of silk came from silk worms, which lived on the leaves taken from mulberry trees grown in the area.

They were very proud, hardworking people and regarded themselves as rich because they had a roof over their heads and food on the table. Their children, family and relatives were with them and they had peace in their lives. They loved their village and the beautiful surrounding country with its lush green mountains, fertile valleys growing their vegetables and fruit, and they grazed their animals in the green fields. The families had lived for many generations in this village.

There was a large tree situated in the centre of the village where many celebrations took place. *A Turkish lady had told me that 'Kouvoukleia' meant 'the tree in the centre', but my Theo (Uncle) Kuriako Deliyannis disagreed. For his Doctorate in 2002, the title of his thesis was, "The idiom of Kouvoukleia, a village of Bursa in Turkey". He found that in the language of Kouvoukleia, an Asian Minor Greek language, which had been spoken for centuries, 'Kouvoukleia' meant 'a canopy'.*

The history of the area is very colourful. The people were descendants of the Aeolians. The Aeolians were Hellenic people from Aeolis and Lesbos in Central Greece who had settled in the West Coast of Asia Minor (now Turkey). By 688 BC the Ionians were the rulers, who were later followed by the Lydians. After the Lydians came Antigonus I, King of Macedonia, then Lysimachus a general in the service of Alexander the Great, and then by the Romans. Kouvoukleia became an early Christian area and from the fourth century AD it was part of the Byzantine Empire until the 15th century and was ruled by the Byzantines and then by the Ottomans. From 1402 it was ruled by the Turkic conqueror Tamarlane, and after 1424 it belonged to the Ottoman Turks.

The village of Kouvoukleia was one of the last to fall into Ottoman hands. And the reason was because of the legend that has been passed down in our family that the village had been very strong in their Christian faith for hundreds of years and had been protected by a man riding a white horse. He was dressed in armour and would ride around the village during the night. They all believed it was St George, as the village had a church that was named after St George, and many would attend this sacred place, particularly on Sundays and on any Saints' Days that they celebrated. It was where they learnt about their faith and about the word of God. Their spiritual guide was St George. He was their strength and protector, and he was their intercessor to God. I heard this legend from my *Thea* (Auntie) Chrissy Avramidis and I was in awe, as often I would hear my *Mama* saying, "St George has been protecting you again".

After the invasion of the Ottoman Turks in the 15th century, life changed for all of them as they had to learn to live peacefully together, Christians and Muslims, Asia Minor Greek and Turkish people. When they celebrated the various feast days of their religions and cooked their special meals they would share them with their neighbours, friends and relatives. They supported and helped each other. My *Baba* often said that as a young child he remembered his *Manna* sharing food with their Muslim neighbours, especially when one of them was not well. For years the inhabitants' great strength was their faith in God, the fellowship that they all shared and the caring they had for each other. For instance, if they were planting or harvesting and a villager was sick, the others would help by coming over to lend a hand to finish planting or to harvest the fields. If a woman was sick, it would be quite common for a neighbour to cook lentil soup or a stew and take it to the family. Other villagers would help by taking various fruits or vegetables to the sick. They had a sense of pride and community spirit. People interacted and enjoyed the fruits of their combined labour.

But this peaceful life changed for Kouvoukleia when the Balkan War broke out on the 18th September, 1912. The Greek Government, with her Balkan allies, declared war on the Ottoman Turks to liberate the downtrodden Christians. Throughout the Ottoman Empire there were many villages and towns where the Christians were persecuted, forbidden to speak their language and practise their faith. For Kouvoukleia this was not the case as the majority of the people were Asia Minor Greek Christians and they lived peacefully with their neighbours, the Muslims. But soon things changed and neighbours could not trust each other. Life became unbearable for all of them.

#1
The Blessing

Gianni's parents were Malamati and Athanasis Rizougloudzins. They were people who were very proud of their heritage and traditions. The villagers who were Christians spoke an Asia Minor Greek language; the Muslims spoke Turkish. However, all could also speak or understand Turkish. These people had lived there for hundreds of years and had lived peacefully, but at the start of the 20th century, life in this small village of Kouvoukleia began to change.

On 18th September, 1912 Greece, along with her Balkan allies, declared war on the Ottoman Turks, thus beginning the First Balkan War. The aim of the Greek Government led by Eleftherios Venizelos was to improve the living conditions of the Christian population and to liberate them. But unfortunately, the conditions only worsened not only for the people in Kouvoukleia, but all those throughout Asia Minor (Ottoman Turkey).

The people from Greece, Turkey and the Balkan League countries began to suffer an unimaginably horrible holocaust of terror and suffering, as they became refugees. Thousands died in the cold, from disease and starvation. The bloodthirsty armies of looters and rapists massacred innocent people. People were afraid that they had lost their freedom. Where neighbours once helped each other and encouraged one another, life was now completely different. The Ottoman Turkish army destroyed the church of St George in Kouvoukleia, and the people were forbidden to practise their faith.

The times were turbulent. Even though Muslims and Christians had lived peacefully together for many centuries in Kouvoukleia, the situation had changed and now they could not trust each other. When the authorities from Prousa were looking for renegades or Christians, they arrested Athanasis as he was a strong Christian and one of the leaders of the village.

Anyone who the Ottoman Turkey authorities deemed to be a threat, or who was against their beliefs, disappeared. Men were taken away and never seen again. They were imprisoned or used for hard labor in building roads or bridges. This happened throughout the country. Such was the case with Athanasis, Gianni's *Baba,* who was a Christian and very strong in his Christian faith. At the time all the villagers were appalled, as Athanasis was always ready to help others and their faith or belief did not matter to him as he respected and cared for everyone.

All the families were afraid to ask where he had been taken, or where he was, in fear of causing more problems, so they all kept quiet. He had simply disappeared. Gianni's *Manna* Malamati was afraid to say that she was a Christian from then on for fear of retaliation, as she had three children to look after.

Gianni could not even remember his *Baba*. He wished he still had his *Baba* as other boys did. He had taken the role of supporting the family at a young age. He was still a child, but was working from sunrise to sunset in the fields. He planted and harvested the vegetables for their food. It was backbreaking work, especially for one so young, but they had to survive and, as Gianni was the eldest child, he took the role of his *Baba* as provider and protector of his family. His *Giagia* (paternal grandmother) and *Manna* (mother) ran the silk factory downstairs.

Gianni was not sure how old he was. Many of the Christians knew their age by their baptism certificates. However, the church where their baptism records were kept had been destroyed. All of the villagers were told by the Ottoman Turkish authorities to go to the town centre and be registered regardless of whether they had their baptism certificates or not. The Ottoman authorities refused to recognise any of their Christian papers. In 1915 everyone had to be registered as war was raging in Gallipoli and the authorities wanted all young men to be used either to carry supplies, build roads or to join the army.

Although Gianni did not know the exact date of his birth, his birth certificate (issued by the Ottomans) now showed that he was born in May 1912. But his brother and younger sister also had the same date, even though he was a few years older than his brother Christopher and sister Despina. *Theo* (Uncle) Thanaso Solomidis, who was Gianni's cousin (their mothers were sisters), told me when Gianni died... "*Your Baba was older than all of us. When we all went to be registered, they put the birthday dates that they felt the person was on all of our birth certificates. It did not matter to them how old we were.*" He thought that Gianni was probably born very early in the 19th century.

Gianni worked in the fields all day harvesting the hay with a sickle then tying it in bundles, putting it on a cart and storing it in the barn. It was very hard working all day out in the sun. His hands were blistered, but he knew he could not give up. Gianni had to work hard in the fields growing all their vegetables and produce, to help his *Manna* feed the family. He was the eldest, the man in the family.

Gianni loved the animals – the horse, mule, goats and the chickens, and after working in the fields all day he also had to feed and water them. This meant that he had to fetch water from the communal spring water tap in the centre of the village. He made sure that the animals were all cleaned and cared for; it was his last chore for the day. Gianni loved relaxing in his *Giagia's* barn after he had fed the animals. He loved the smell of the clean hay. The animals were kept at his paternal *Giagia's* house as at his house the women worked in the silk workshop under the house.

At the end of the day he would often lie down in the hay, relaxing and thinking that if his *Baba* was home things would be different. He would probably be going to school like his brother, cousins and friends. This was his time to relax and dream '*If only, if only things were different*'. He knew if he went home, his *Manna* would find things for him to do. There was always work to be done. This was his rest time, away from his younger sister, brother and his *Manna,* as he was so tired after working in the field all day and needed to rest.

Gianni often wondered where his *Baba* was, what prison did the Ottoman authorities take him to? Was he still alive or was he dead? No-one knew. And no-one dared to ask for they too would be in trouble.

One day as Gianni relaxed in the fresh hay in the loft he heard people talking. He listened. He recognized his *Giagia's* voice, but there was also a man's voice that he could not recognise. Who was his *Giagia* talking to? Gianni was very curious and he crawled to the edge of the loft and tried to look and listen, but he nearly slipped and fell. He grabbed the ladder just in time to save himself from falling.

"Who's that?"The man demanded. His *Giagia* and the man looked up.

"It is all right, it is all right, it is only Giannko, your son. Giannko, come down and meet your *Baba*."

When Gianni looked down he saw a tall man whose bones were showing through the rags that he was wearing. He was filthy. He did not want to know this man. His clothes were torn, they were tattered and hanging off him. He could not possibly be his *Baba* as he could smell him from the top of the ladder. This man had not washed for years. Gianni thought to himself '*What was his Giagia talking about? She must be going mad in her old age*'. This could not be his *Baba*; he never ever dreamt that his *Baba* would be in rags. Gianni slowly came down the ladder and watched them. This man was very tall with long, wavy, black hair that had never been combed, a dirty beard and moustache that had never been washed and yet his *Giagia* had hugged him and kissed him. What was wrong with her? She beckoned him, "Giannko come and meet your *Baba*".

Gianni slowly walked to them and stared. Could this man really be his *Baba?* The man approached and lifted Gianni and hugged him, saying "My son, my son. *H Dunami Tou Theou Na Ine Pandode mazi sou"*. (May God's strength be always with you.) He kissed Gianni, hugged him once more and ran out into the dark night in case the Ottoman Turks came looking for him. That was the first and last recollection that Gianni had of his *Baba*. But this was his secret; this was the gift that his *Baba* had blessed him with and he treasured it throughout his life.

Athanasis did not go to see his wife as he was sure that the authorities would be watching out for him at her house. So he had gone to see his *Manna* for help as he needed clothes and food.

Gianko's *Giagia* said to him, "Giannko, do not mention this to anyone,. especially your *Manna,* brother or sister. They must not know that my son has escaped the Ottoman Turkish prison or they will be punished. This is our secret. Your *Baba* has escaped from the Ottoman prison in Prousa. Only God knows where he will find sanctuary and safety. I have given him food and clothes, but that will only keep him going for a little while. Where he will find help I do not know; only God knows". That was Gianni's secret; his *Baba's* blessing carried him through his life. It was his secret, and it was his *Baba's* gift.

A couple of days later when Gianni arrived home from the fields he found two tall Turkish men from Bursa. They were the Ottoman authorities who had come looking for Athanasis, his *Baba*. They were trashing the house. His *Manna* was hugging his younger brother and sister while huddled together in a corner. They wanted to know where she had hidden her husband. Gianni's *Manna*, Malamati, was yelling, "I have not seen my husband for years; you should know where he is, you had taken him away. An innocent man that was always ready to help others, his blood is in your hands". Malamati always had to voice her opinion.

"You dare to talk to us like that. We will teach you a lesson, woman". They yelled at her and then the taller one grabbed Malamati by the hair and dragged her and kicked the two younger children, savagely, back in the corner. Gianni watched from the doorway, horrified, unable to do anything.

The Turks grabbed coals from the grate and threw them on to the floor and then made Malamati walk on the hot coals, each one pushing her back and forward on the coals as they laughed. When they had had their fun they pushed Gianni against the wall and walked out, laughing and joking to each other. Everything inside their home was left behind in ruins. Malamati hugged the children as she fell on the floor crossing herself, crying and thanking H *Panagia* (the mother of God) that they were all still alive. At least they were safe for the time being.

Gianni tried to salvage what he could, cleaning and tidying the house. He gently applied some yoghurt on Malamati's feet to take the pain away and then helped her to bandage her feet with old tea towels that he soaked in chamomile tea. Gianni then helped his younger brother and sister, who were crying in pain and fear, as the man who had kicked them had inflicted terrible wounds on them; he cleaned the wounds and then bandaged their wounds up. Malamati was thankful that they were not raped or killed and kept crossing herself and thanking the mother of God.

The Ottomans left Malamati and her children empty-handed, not finding Athanasis. Gianni looked after his mother, brother and sister cleaning their wounds with the help of his *Giagia*. Life had become very unbearable as they were worried that the authorities could trouble them again.

At the end of the World War I and after the collapse of the Ottoman Empire, the governments of Greece and the new country, Turkey, both agreed to the exchange of their people. The Muslims and the Christians were to be relocated. The Muslims in Greece were to be relocated to Turkey while the Greek Christians in Turkey were to be relocated to Greece, each leaving behind homes and lands that their families had owned for generations. Unfortunately many innocent people were killed on both sides during this exchange.

In 1922 the first exodus from Kouvoukleia took place. The villagers had to leave behind their homes, animals, precious possessions and everything they had worked for all their lives. They had no time to pack. They were told by the Ottoman authorities from Prousa to leave or they would be killed. They grabbed what they could, wrapped everything in a sheet and fled with their few belongings and left the lands and homes that had been in their families for many generations. Gianni remembered his paternal grandmother throwing the belongings she could not carry into a well hoping that in time they might return and recover them. She then tearfully locked her home. Some of those homes are still locked and have remained empty until the present time. He remembered his *Manna* putting all her jewellery on, especially the three strings of Flouria (gold coins) that she wore around her neck; it was her husband's present to her on their wedding day.

Malamati's parents were very well off, and had given the house as her dowry. They had a thriving silk industry. Athanasis' parents had a home silk industry also at Kouvoukleia and they would often come and trade their handiwork with Malamati's parents. The parents had arranged their marriage. As Athanasis was one of the leaders of Kouvoukleia they felt that their daughter would be looked after, as he was also a hard-working man. They were sure that their daughter had a wonderful husband and he would look after her.

Malamati, with her brothers and sisters, had been taught to read and write. They had never worked in the fields, but had helped their parents, Hlia and Efrepia (Pespoules) Deliyannis, with their silk industry. When they were young they would travel to Constantinople or Smryna with their parents to sell all their handicrafts, especially at the Grand Bazaar with its thousands of shops. They loved walking through all the shops as they enjoyed shopping and mixing with all the crowds. Malamati often reminisced about the smells of spices and delicacies of all the food shops. Her mouth would water as she remembered the wonderful food, and she would say, "One could buy anything their heart desired in the Grand Bazaar in Constantinople". She especially enjoyed visiting her eldest sister who had married a Turkish businessman who owned one of the shops at the Grand Bazaar. Her elder sister would often spoil them with many gifts to take back home. But her parents were never happy with their older daughter marrying a Muslim as she had changed her faith. Especially when the war broke out they disowned her and had forbidden the children to mention her name.

Malamati and her siblings were all taught to run the silk business. For Malamati to work in the fields was unheard of. She had been spoilt and had never worked out in the sun. Malamati enjoyed designing and running her home silk industry. But her world had collapsed when she lost her husband, and now to leave everything behind was devastating. Whatever they owned and treasured could not be taken with them. They had no choice, they had to flee for their lives.

Gianni put his *Manna,* with his brother (Christopher) and sister (Despina), on the mule and packed some food and whatever they could carry wrapped in a sheet. They locked their house, hoping that they would return one day, and left. Other villagers who resisted in any way were either shot or taken away.

The Christian population of Asia Minor fled, including all the Greek Christians from the village of Kouvoukleia. Gianni and his *Manna,* his brother and sister and all the relatives fled across the mountains to the port of Moudania (now known as Mudanya), approximately 25 kilometres from Kouvoukleia taking with them only what they could carry.

The Turkish authorities from Prousa told the Christians that they would be compensated for the lands and homes they left behind. They would find their *Promised Land*, as the Greek Government was to help them. They were born and had lived in the village of Kouvoukleia all their lives. To leave everything behind, home, lands and animals was heart- wrenching. Where would this *Promised Land* be?

Those who were strong, and able to, scrambled on to the Greek fishing boats at the port of Moudania. Many were massacred or drowned trying to escape. The water was red with the blood from those who had been slaughtered. There were bodies everywhere. The lucky ones made it to the Greek fishing boats to be taken to Greece, the country that was to be their *Promised Land*. Many died from starvation and the bitter cold or were shot by the many renegades or the Turkish soldiers as they fled.

On the 13th August, 1922 Mustafa Kamel Ataturk launched an attack on the Greek front at Afion Karahisar and within 14 days the Turks entered Smyrna and put it to the torch, having slaughtered the Greek population of the area. The foreign forces of England, America and France watched the dreadful catastrophe unfold from their warships anchored off Smyrna without intervening. Their governments had instructed them to assist only their own people.

Hundreds of thousands of people were taken to Athens, Thessaloniki or the many islands, but the people in Greece were suffering from the many wars already and did not want all these people arriving. There was not enough food for themselves and to help these thousands of people arriving on their doorstep, who were suffering from malnutrition, together with the sick and wounded, was a huge task. The Greeks were appalled and disgusted with their Government. They needed help to feed these people who were arriving in their thousands. The Government was not able to provide that help as the country had been ravaged by the many wars.

Under Eleftherios Venizelos, the Greek Government signed the treaty of Lausanne with Turkey on 24 July, 1923. Under this treaty another million Christians were expelled from Turkey (in exchange for 500,000 Muslims who had lived in Greece). There were one and a half million Asian Minor Greek Christians who fled for their lives from Turkey into Greece from 1922 to 1923.

#2
Exodus from Turkey

G*iagia* Malamati would often tell me of the atrocities that the war created, with innocent people suffering, being raped, tortured and killed. Refugees from Turkey were robbed and murdered by brigands. Others drank stagnant water, got swamp fever or died in refugee camps from typhoid, malaria, or lack of food or medications.

After a horrendous journey through the waters of the Aegean Sea where many died in the overcrowded boats because of their injuries, lack of food, sanitation and medication, they arrived in Piraeus, the port for Athens. Others landed in Thessaloniki in northern Greece. All my *Baba's* relatives stayed together and were taken to a refugee camp outside Thessaloniki where my *Baba's* sister, Despina, died. It was a horrible time for all of them. The two boys watched their *Manna* nursing their sister, and as she died slowly in their *Manna's* arms they all cried and Malamati kept praying to God for a miracle. The refugees had no food, clothes, water, medications or sanitation and they had terrible weather conditions. Many roamed the countryside looking for greens (mainly weeds) to cook and begged for food daily. These people who once had their own homes had now been turned into beggars through no fault of their own. Sometimes Malamati would exchange one of her gold coins for any food or even for a loaf of bread.

The cold winds and wet weather often kept them in their makeshift shelters. Many died in those shelters as they all huddled together to try and keep warm. Whole families were often found dead in their shelters. The army just buried hundreds of them, unidentified. They all waited for Government assistance and for the authorities to relocate them to their new homes, but the Government was in a very bad financial situation and was unable to help the refugees. Malamati and her relatives were eventually sent to the village of Mahala in northern Greece, near the town of Florina, and were allocated old Muslim homes. As these homes had been empty for a long time they often needed cleaning and painting, but those people who were given the homes felt privileged as they now had a roof over their heads and were sheltered from the weather. These were the homes that had been owned by the Muslims who had been sent to Turkey while the Greek Asian Minor Christians had been evicted from Turkey and sent to Greece, due to the "Agreed Exchange" by both countries.

There were not enough houses to give to all of the refugees, so many built new villages, especially in the north of Greece. There were 300 of these refugee villages across northern Greece that sprang up. Many people who had come from the same village in Turkey tried to stay together. When they built new villages they named them after the villages that they had left from in Asia Minor Turkey, for example, the village of Nea Moudania in Greece (the new Moudania), or Examile, where my brother's best man and his wife (Theodoros and Eudoxia Diamandopoulos) and their people had come from, after the village of Examile in Asia Minor.

They all worked hard and built the new villages. Groups of families and friends stayed together so that they could help and rebuild their lives again. All of Malamati's relatives were together to help, encourage and care for each other. She just followed her brother and sister-in-law, Mersina and Parashos Deliyannis and his family, her mother Efrepia who lived with her brother Parashos and her sister's family, Anastasia and Christos Solomidis. Malamati felt safe being with her brother and sister as her husband Athanasis was never found and her *Baba,* Hlia Deliyannis, died in the refugee camp.

Mahala is six kilometres from the town of Florina in northern Greece. It is an alpine area and a very beautiful part of Greece, although extremely cold. In winter the temperatures could plummet to minus 20°C. The mountains were often covered with snow for three to four months of the year.

The village of Mahala's name was changed in the 1930's to Tropaioukhos, after the little church in the village, which was named after St George Tropaioukhoros.

In this village seven different dialects were spoken. There were refugees from all over the Ottoman Empire. The Greek Government wanted them all to go to school and learn the Greek language as some of them could only speak a combination of Greek and Turkish, Pontus, Asia Minor Greek, Macedonian or different dialects. Those who did not agree to learn the Greek language were persecuted or imprisoned.

The house that Malamati was allocated was a two-storey Turkish house built from mud bricks and had long, thin windows. Malamati, Gianni and his brother, Christopher, lived upstairs where there were two bedrooms, a living and kitchen room, while downstairs was the barn where the animals lived. They were allocated a few parcels of land to grow their food. Gianni worked hard with his mother and brother for the first few years in the village, trying to improve their lives. However, in order for them to improve their living conditions they needed more land.

Married couples had priority when more land was allocated. Malamati said to her son, "Giannko, you have to get married in order for us to receive more land".

"*Manna,* you cannot find a woman just like that," Giannko said.

"Giannko, there are so many young women in the village; tell me who you like. I will go and ask her parents if she is willing to marry you."

"*Manna* I will find one, don't worry," Giannko said.

"You better hurry as the Government is allocating land and we don't want to miss out," Malamati said.

In 1932, officially Gianni was 20 years old, but he was probably in his mid to late 20s. As his *Manna* often said that he was born in 1906 and not 1912, but she was not sure of the exact date. As babies were not registered in those days, only when the baby was baptised the date was registered in the church, but the baby could have been two to three years old or older. But unfortunately the church and all the records had been destroyed.

Giannko wondered how he would find a young lady just like that. He never went to any Saints' Day's dances or celebrations that the village held. All Gianni did was work and work. But he knew that he had to get married in order to be allocated more land.

When the family had extra produce, Gianni would take it to sell at the markets in Florina. He could then buy salt, soap, sugar, oil and other necessities for the family's daily needs. As there was no shop or supermarket in the village they all had to grow their vegetables, fruit, grapes, wheat, tobacco, and make their butter, cheese, yoghurt, pickles, jams and wine. They were all self-sufficient and all their produce was stored in their cellars for the whole year. The garlands of garlic and onions were hung to dry and they stored their wheat, corn, pickles, cheeses, jams, wines and tsipouro (home-brew spirit). Gianni loved the markets, the noisy atmosphere of the stallkeepers and crowds; he especially loved the sweet smells of baklavas, galaktobouriko (custard pie), melomacarona (honey cookies), halvas, spanakopita and the many sweets and delicatessen produce. And he loved to buy fresh fish to take home as it was a treat to have now and then as his *Manna* loved fresh fish.

One particular day he took his produce to the markets in Florina. As Gianni had finished selling his produce to the stallkeepers, he spotted a young lady walking slowly through the market, dragging her feet. She had a lovely, long, brown plait of hair. Her head was bowed and she seemed to be crying. Gianni wondered what was wrong with her, but thought to himself *"Yes, that is the lady I am going to marry"*, so he followed her around as she was walking through the marketplace. He thought that he would find out where she lived and then send his *Manna* to her parents asking for their permission for her son to marry their daughter. It would be a proxy marriage, as the parents would arrange the marriage rather than the couple.

The young lady's name was Olga. She hung her head to hide the tears she shed as she remembered the headmaster's announcement that morning at the college. The Government could not afford to keep the college going in Florina. There were not enough students wanting to continue college so it was closing down, relocating and combining with another college in a larger town. Those students who wanted to continue had to see the headmaster. In 1932 students would finish primary school, which was the first six years of their schooling, and then they would attend a college for four years to be primary school teachers. She had already completed two years at the college and she needed another two years to finish as a teacher.

Olga was extremely upset. How could she go to another town? Her parents could not afford it. Her thoughts were in turmoil as she wandered through the markets. Olga wondered how her parents could possibly send her to another town. They were refugees from Margarra in Thraki, Turkey, who had been uprooted from their home and were struggling to survive.

Olga's parents were old and had suffered losing their home and their six sons in the exchange. The elder two boys were killed when the Turkish soldiers come through their village, killing anyone in their path. These were innocent young boys, who were playing in the street as their grandparents were watching them. The old, the young children and women and men who were in the soldiers' path were all massacred. The rest of the village had all grabbed whatever they could and fled their village.

Their memories and losses were painful and they tried not to remember that the Turkish soldiers had grabbed one set of their twins and threw them in the water as they tried to get on to the fishing boats. The other set of twins had died in the refugee camps. They hoped for a better future for their daughters and not to endure the pain that they had suffered. They at least had a roof over their heads and there was food on the table for their daughters. Olga's parents were struggling to bring up the three younger daughters.

They were pleased that their eldest daughter, Giannoulla, had married. She was very pretty and they were happy when an older man had asked for her hand and did not ask for a dowry. He was 30 years older than her, but at least they had one less mouth to feed. They were hoping that each daughter would be able to marry as well as Giannoulla had done. They also knew that they had to provide each one with a dowry, but that would be impossible for them.

Olga's *Manna,* Olympia, worked in a bakery while her *Baba*, Zacharia Houvarda, was a naturopath and chiropractor. Zacharia found that helping people was not easy as not many people could afford to pay with cash. Some would pay with a chicken or bread or vegetables, not like his clinic in Margarra, Thraki, where people would pay him in cash. He had lost everything, but still he and Olympia were thankful to have the little that they had.

Olga dragged her feet as she walked up and down through the stalls of the markets trying to think of a way out of her problem, and how she would tell her parents, but all she could see was a bleak future. Deep down she knew that there was no possibility of attending college any more

She walked around and around. Gradually the stallkeepers were packing up and were heading home for their siesta. Olga reluctantly headed home. It was getting late and the streets were deserted during siesta.

As Olga walked towards home she noticed that a young man was following her and she wondered where he was going and what he was up to. Olga's house was a small cottage along a path on the edge of town. It was on the side of a mountain with a creek flowing past their street. As there was no access past their door (unless one wanted to climb the mountain) people used the road, and did not come along this pathway. Olga stopped and looked back before opening her front door. She met

Gianni's dark eyes for a few seconds. His eyes were brown with a glint of mischief in them. He was tall with black, wavy hair and he smiled at her, gently bending his head to one side. He then turned and walked back along the old dirt path. Olga walked in quickly, closed the door, and then looked out the window curious as to who the young man might be.

"What's wrong?" Olga's younger sister, Sapfo, asked as she joined Olga at the window.

"I could be mistaken, but I am sure that a man followed me home."

"Oh Olga, isn't that wonderful? You have an admirer!" Sapfo said wistfully.

#3
The Proxy

My *Baba* told me that he would always remember the very first time he saw my *Mama*. He said that he had fallen in love with her from the first time he set eyes on her beautiful, round face and especially her long, flowing plait, in the marketplace.

Gianni was very excited as he headed back to pick up his mule and cart from the markets; he was so happy as he thought of the lovely young lady. He kept thinking, 'Yes, I will marry her'. He was a very proud man. He always worked hard and even though he had no schooling he knew that he could provide for her. He knew that he would make this lady very happy. And he could visualise having children with this young lady and yes, he would look after them. He was pleased that he had followed her. Gianni had made up his mind. He was certain that his Manna would go and arrange everything with the parents of the lovely young lady with the long, brown, flowing plait so that the marriage could take place.

The next day Gianni sent his Manna to ask the young lady's parents' permission to marry her. She went on foot to Florina. Malamati was a strong woman and strode quickly. She always wore long, black clothes and a head scarf, as was the custom, because she had lost her husband and her daughter had died. The black attire made her look like a crow ready for the kill. Malamati often said that she was fuming with her son as she followed the directions that he had given her to visit the young lady's parents in the house at the edge of Florina. As she headed down the dirt path to find the house her son had described she was thinking to herself "There were so many hard-working, eligible girls in the village. But no! Gianni had to be different! He had found a city girl who had no knowledge of village life and who would twirl him around her little finger!" What was she going to say to these people? Malamati was not one to be short of words and to actually admit that she was not sure what to say to them seemed incredulous. She was one who called a spade a spade and would simply come out with words, whether she hurt one's feelings or not.

By midmorning Malamati had reached the house. She knocked at the door. A young girl with a long plait opened the door and said politely, "Can I help you, Kuria (Mrs.)?" Malamati thought that she certainly had manners but hoped that she was also a hard-working girl.

"Yes. I would like to see your *Baba*," Malamati replied abruptly.

"Would you like to come in?" Olga ushered her into the living room. "Sit down and I will get my *Baba*. He is at the back of the house." Olga often said if she knew why she had come that morning she would not have let her in, but she thought that she needed to see her *Baba* for medications as he was an herbalist and naturopath.

While Olga was out of the room Malamati noticed that the little cottage was clean and tidy, but had little in the way of furniture. The living room had three divans on opposite sides of the room and a low, round table in the middle with cushions scattered around it. There were lace curtains on the windows and a rug was on the floor. The place was certainly clean and tidy, even though there were only the basic necessities in the house. However, it was clear that the family was quite poor.

Olga's *Baba* came in and said, "What can I help you with, Kuria?"

Malamati, not one to waste words, replied, “My son, Gianni, saw your daughter at the market and he would like to marry her”.

Zacharia was taken aback with surprise and exclaimed, “Sorry, what did you say?”

“Like I said, I am here for my son. He sent me as a proxy to ask you for your permission to marry your daughter,” Malamati repeated.

“Could you please wait? I’ll go and have a word with my wife Olympia and discuss this with her. I thought you had come because you were sick,” Zacharia said.

“Oh my God, I never get sick, never. I am as strong as a horse. I don’t believe in medications”, Malamati answered abruptly. (The truth was that when she was very young she was sick and a doctor had visited her, as her parents were worried about her. He had given her a yellow mixture to take. It was very bitter and she was determined never to take medications ever again. She then poured this mixture through the hole of the floor and it landed on the mule’s back and her parents had wondered what it was on the mule. She vowed that she would never take medications again!)

“Olga, could you please bring some refreshments?” Zacharia called out to his daughter as he went out of the room to talk to his wife.

Zacharia returned to the room. “I am Zacharia Houvarda and this is my wife Olympia. And you are?”

“I am Malamati Rizidou. (The Greeks have male and female surnames; females end with ‘ou’ and males end their surname with ‘is’.) I have two sons, Gianni and Christopher. I am a widow and I lost my husband in the war with the Turks. In order for us to claim land, my eldest son Gianni must marry. He is a hard-working young man and he will make a good husband. I had asked him to find a girl. He saw your daughter in the markets in Florina and then followed her to your house yesterday. He asked me to come and see you as a proxy, as he must marry straight away in order to apply for more land. We live in the village of Tropaioukhos.” Malamati ended her sales pitch.

Olympia said, “I will call my daughter in and ask her.”

Olga came in bringing a tray of homemade gliko (fig with roasted almonds) preserve and glasses of cold water.

"Olga, this lady has an eligible son. He saw you yesterday and he would like to marry you. He is a strong, young, hard-working man. What do you think?"

Even though Zacharia asked Olga for her thoughts he didn't wait for an answer. Olga's parents and Malamati went ahead and planned Olga's life.

Olga nearly dropped the tray. Her *Baba* grabbed it and put the tray on the low table. Olga collapsed on to the divan devastated, thinking "How could they do this? This must be a nightmare". But she listened as her parents and Malamati organised her life for her. There would not have been any point complaining or arguing. In those days children were raised to do exactly what their parents told them to do.

Zacharia said, "Kuria Malamati, you must realise that we are refugees from the old country. I have no dowry to give with our daughter".

"Don't worry about that because I have suffered too, losing my husband, my daughter, home and lands in that terrible war. They were horrible times. Now we must look forward to building our lives again," Malamati said.

"Yes, we too lost sons, our home and lands, but we managed to flee to save ourselves and rebuild our lives again. That is why there is no dowry," explained Zacharia.

Malamati was not perturbed. "That is fine. But they must get married straight away. They will manage. They are young. They can get married on Sunday when a lot of other couples are being married."

Malamati asked them "Are you agreeable for our children to marry? If so, they must marry on Sunday. The service starts at 10 o'clock in the morning at St George's Church in Tropaioukhos. Just bring your daughter there."

Zacharia replied, "My wife and I are honoured. I am happy that you are also from the old country like us. It is a pleasure for our children to be married, especially people who have gone through many adversities like us, but come through it all". The proxy transaction was concluded when each ate the sweets and then washed them down with the cold water.

They all shook hands and Malamati left. Zacharias looked at his daughter and said excitedly "Olga, my daughter, this is a godsend. I cannot afford to send you to the college, but you can marry. This is a young, hard-working man and he's from the old country."

"*Baba*, I don't know him. You don't know him! How can I marry him?" Olga protested, "How can you do this to me?" She was fuming.

"Olga, I didn't know your *Baba*, but I married him," Olympia reasoned with her daughter.

"*Mama*, times have changed. Surely you don't expect me to marry him!"

Olympia said gently "Olga, you will learn to love him, have children and care for each other. Do not be afraid. H Dunami Tou Theou na ine pandode mazi sou. (May God's strength be always with you)".

Zacharia explained, "My child, I have no dowry to give to you. Who would marry you?"

"What's wrong with you, *Baba*?" You married off my eldest sister, Gianoulla, at the age of 17 to a rich man who is 30 years older than her. An old man! Now you want to marry me at 14 years of age to a poor farmer. And Sapfo, are you going to marry her to a beggar man at 10 years old? And what about six-year-old Anna? Why don't you marry her off to a pauper? You must be mad *Baba*? No I will not marry just anyone. Do you hear?"

"Olga, don't speak to your *Baba* like that! Apologise to him!" Olympia yelled at her daughter.

"My daughter... My daughter, I wish I could marry you off to a wealthy man. But I have no means to do that. At least Gianni was attracted to you and he is a hard- working man. And his *Mama* said he is as strong as a bull. That is final. You will do as I say!" her *Baba* said firmly.

Olga was stunned. She could not believe what was happening. She wanted to scream and yell and tell them what they were doing was wrong. It was not fair. However, she knew that her *Baba*'s mind was made up and, by tradition, his word was law in their house as it was in all Greek homes. She had to obey him.

#4
THE WEDDING

Olga had seen Gianni for a few minutes and she wondered if he was kind and would treat her well. What sort of a man was he? All of Olga's belongings were wrapped in a tablecloth. She wondered if all of her dreams were wrapped up in that bundle. They all headed for the village on foot as if they were going on a picnic. Olga was extremely upset about the arrangements, but she had to obey her parents and she went along with their wishes. Olympia had stayed up all night to sew the wedding dress for her daughter. It was nothing spectacular as it was just a plain white calico dress. The preparations and the wedding all took place within a few days. Gianni had seen his prospective bride on Thursday at the market day and the wedding was just three days later, on the Sunday.

Early on Sunday, Olga's family had all washed and dressed in their good clothes. As they walked on foot to Tropaioukhos they were all joking and laughing, except Olga. It was Olga's and Gianni's big day, their wedding day. My parents talked about it later and even they could not believe how it happened so quickly. It was like a dream to them, or as my *Mama* would say '*more like a nightmare*'.

It was over an hour's walk to the village of Tropaioukhos; it is six kilometres from Florina. The day was beautiful and sunny. The little Church of St George at Tropaioukhos was crowded with everyone from the village and many from Florina. The candles were all lit and each icon shined as if blessing the congregation. The atmosphere was serene. Everyone was happy except Olga, who was seething. She knew that she could not go against her *Baba*'s wishes and she tried to make some sense of all that was happening.

The bride's sister, Sapfo, was always curious, so when she asked "Where did all these people come from? Are they all here for Olga's wedding?" Olga felt like throttling her.

"No, my child the Government is issuing land to people if they are married. Lots of young couples are getting married today so that they can claim land," replied her father,"

Each couple in turn was married. When the priest came to Olga and Gianni, the priest stated, "Olga is too young. She cannot get married as she is only 14. The service cannot take place".

Gianni's mother, Malamati, glared at the priest, and said, "*Pater* (Father), you will marry them and we will put down that she is 18 years old. I don't know what the fuss is about as I was only 14 when I got married". So they entered into the marriage register that my mother was born in 1914 instead of 1918.

The marriage ceremony was a very simple one with Olga's parents, Zacharia and Olympia, and her sisters Sapfo and Anna, together with Gianni's *Manna*, Malamati, and his brother Christopher attending. Their *koubarri* (best man) Eustratios and Stratia Koutsoubithou with their family, their father Fragoulis and their children were also there. And many of Gianni's cousins from the Deliyannis and Solomidis families were also there.

Gianni was pleased, as Olga looked beautiful on their wedding day, but she did look sad. Gianni had worn his only good trousers and a new woven shirt. He had polished his shoes, and for once they were actually shining.

At every household there were small celebrations for the various weddings. There was a small gathering at Malamati's house after the service to celebrate the young couple's marriage. They had *mezethes* (nibbles) to eat, home-brewed wine and the *tsipouro* (spirits) to drink, all of which had been prepared by Malamati. They all wished the young couple well and then Olga's parents and sisters left and walked back to Florina.

Olga was miserable and all alone with strangers when her parents left. She felt hurt and deserted. Her new husband Gianni was never much of a talker; Olga often said it seemed that she had to drag words out of Gianni's mouth with a crochet hook.

Although Gianni did not say much, his *Manna* made up for him. She certainly was in control of the household as Olga soon found out. If anyone spoke, it would be Malamati, who spoke for everyone. Gianni would smile at his young wife every now and then and Olga wondered how in the world she was going to fall in love with this man. Her *Mama* had talked to her and told her that "Eventually you will fall in love with your husband and have children". Olga hoped that like her mother she also would eventually fall in love with this man who kept on smiling at her.

#5
Life in the Village

My *Giagia* Malamati lived with us in later times when we had moved to Melbourne, Australia, and often *Mama* and her mother-in-law would talk about the old times. *Mama* would say to her that she certainly was hard on her when she first got married. *Giagia* Malamati would reply "But you learned that way, didn't you?" And then they would argue about old times. Their lives were very hard back then. There were no modern conveniences or luxuries and they often wondered how they made it through each day. *Mama* often said, "It was only with God's strength and courage that we come through all our ordeals".

Olga had not only become the wife of Gianni, but she had also become housekeeper to her mother-in-law, Malamati, and also to Gianni's brother, Christopher. There was no honeymoon – it was straight to work for Olga!

The day after the wedding was the hardest day in Olga's life. She was young and did not know what to do. She had spent much of the night tossing and turning while her husband slept. The mattress was made out of straw and each time Olga moved the straw stuck into her. She wished she had her own divan from Florina, which was made from shredded rags. After staying awake for much of the night, Olga finally managed to fall asleep. It was the sun that woke her up. Gianni had got up very early and went off to the fields, but he had left her a jug of water, a bowl and a face washer by the bed.

Olga freshened up, dressed and then went into the living room. She was tired, and not knowing what to expect, extremely nervous. The room had a couple of divans against the wall. Olga wondered if that was where Christopher may have slept. There was a second door leading to another room where, Olga assumed, that Malamati slept. In the living room was a table with four chairs made out of cane. A long, narrow window let the early morning sunrays into the room. In the sunlight Olga could see that the old combustion stove used for cooking and heating was dusty and was covered in ash. In fact, ash was everywhere. Olga thought that her parents' home was not any better than this, but at least it had crocheted curtains on the windows and the rooms were clean and tidy. But this place needed a thorough clean.

Olga's solitude was broken when Malamati saw her and said, "It's about time! The men have gone in the fields but, being Monday, we do our washing". With that she handed Olga a big basket of washing.

"Where do I do the washing?" Olga asked quietly. At her home, they would carry the water from the creek to a big wooden tub in the kitchen where they would do the washing. The washing water would then be used to water the vegetable garden.

Malamati burst out laughing and shaking her head, exclaimed, "You silly girl. At the river. Where else would you wash?" Olga was despondent, but took the basket and went out the door muttering a little prayer, "God! Please help me".

Olga noticed other women walking along carrying washing baskets so she followed them. They were chatting and laughing with each other. They reached the river where they all sorted out the clothes and washed, chatted and laughed. Olga felt left out, but she followed their movements. She was horrified when suddenly she saw that one of her garments was floating down the river. She realised it was Malamati's bloomers! As she tried to rescue them she fell into the water. The other women burst out laughing and Olga laughed with them. The ice was broken and she introduced herself and came to know some of the women washing. By falling into the river she also lost her soap.

When Olga had finished the washing she piled the cleaned and wet clothes into the basket to take them back home. The basket was very heavy. As she finally managed to get home, she was wet and tired. She saw a rope line in the yard with a long pole in the middle. Olga thought that this was where she should hang out all the clothes, but then she noticed that the men's boxer shorts and singlets, which were originally white, had blotches of black! Malamati's clothes were all black so all the other clothes had turned black. Olga was so annoyed she could not believe herself. Why didn't she take note of that when she commenced the wash?

So she hung Malamati's clothes on the line and then piled all the other clothes back in the basket and returned to the river to wash them again. As she was washing them her tears were flowing and she scrubbed and scrubbed, but her efforts were futile. She took them back and hung them on the rope line. But it was obvious that the clothes were badly stained. She wanted the earth to open up and swallow her.

She noticed Malamati standing at the door of the house. "What have you done, you silly girl? I told my son to find a hard-working village girl! But no, he wanted you. He fell in love with your long plait. We better soak those clothes to whiten them again." Olga gathered the clothes and threw them into a boiler that Malamati had brought out. Olga was fuming by now and ready to leave and return to her parents' home. Malamati placed the boiler on two bricks out in the yard and then put the firewood underneath and said, "Now can you light a fire, girl?"

"Yes", Olga replied.

Malamati gave her the matches and said, "I had better check the *fassoulatha* (bean soup) and I will bring some soda and ash to put into the boiler so we can soak these clothes and whiten them. Before you light the fire go to the village tap and fetch some water. Quickly! The tap is opposite the school". It was about a kilometre from the house.

Olga raced back and forth carrying water from the only tap in the village. The tap was in the centre of the village and was used by the villagers for drinking and washing themselves. It was also where the animals were watered.

When Olga had filled the boiler she thought that she had better light the fire under the boiler. While carrying the water the matches got wet and Olga tried in vain to light the fire. She struck match after match, but also the timber was too thick and the more she tried the more frustrated she got. She had nearly used up all the matches when Malamati came back. "You stupid girl! Give me those matches! You've nearly used a month's supply." Malamati looked around and found some thin sticks and some dry leaves. She put them under the thick wood and lit them. The fire started immediately.

"It only takes one spark to light a fire, like the spark of love you ignited in my son's heart". That was said quietly by Malamati to herself.

At dinner Olga found she was so exhausted she almost fell asleep at the table and was only able to eat a few mouthfuls before she crawled into bed leaving the washing-up to be done by Gianni and Christopher. That night Olga slept like a log. She didn't care what the bed was like.

The next morning, loud banging on her door awoke her, as Malamati yelled at her "Get up! The men have gone to the fields. We have to bake the bread and the sun is already halfway up in the sky". Olga was so sore that she could hardly move. She ached all over and her hands were blistered badly from rubbing the rough clothes the previous day. She found the jug of water, the bowl and the face washer again. She freshened up and dressed quickly, went to the living room and asked, "What can I do?"

"Don't tell me that you don't know how to bake bread, either!" Malamati yelled at her.

Olga began to cry, but Malamati ignored the tears.

"Here is the yeast and the large bag of flour and we bake once a week here," Malamati said. Then she showed Olga the outside brick oven. "You have to light the oven and while it is heating you prepare the bread. I have to go to the fields. You make sure we have enough bread for a week." Olga looked at the oven, sat down and continued to cry.

The tears were rolling down her cheeks when a lady from over the low rock fence next-door called out to her "Olga, are you all right? Can I help? I am your *Thea* (Auntie) Mersina". (Olga found out later that all the neighbours around them were related to Malamati.) *Thea* Mersina was married to Malamati's brother, Parasho Deliyannis.

"I need to light the oven and bake the bread and I don't know how. I just do not know what to do," Olga spluttered.

"Come, I will show you. And don't pay any attention to your mother-in-law. She bosses her sons around and thinks that she can do that to a pretty young lady. Although she yells, she does not mean any harm." And *Thea* Mersina showed Olga step-by-step how to bake bread and clean the house. "To tell you the truth," said *Thea* Mersina, "my sister-in-law hates housekeeping. Gianni or Christopher usually do some housework around the place. Malamati likes to talk and spend time arguing with her brother or sister about politics."

That evening they had delicious fresh bread, which they all enjoyed. As well as baking the bread Olga had cleaned and dusted the entire house. She had even found a clay jug and filled it with some flowers she found growing in the yard. For the first time Olga had felt confident, thanks to *Thea* Mersina.

Christopher complimented her on the clean house and the fresh bread, Gianni just smiled at her, while Malamati grunted an acknowledgment but said nothing.

Life in the village was governed by what day of the week it was. Monday was washing day and Tuesday was spent baking bread. For the rest of the week all worked in the fields from dawn until dark. They harvested and picked vegetables and fruit and tended their vineyards. Women usually pickled vegetables and preserved or prepared food.

Apples, apricots and tomatoes all had to be cleaned, cut in half and dried out in the sun. Nothing was wasted.

At night they all worked by the kerosene lamps threading tobacco leaves for drying, or cleaning corn.

The days were long and the work was hard. There was no electricity or running water in the houses. They used kerosene lamps, and drinking water had to be carried from the only tap in the middle of the village. Water ran continuously from that tap. It came from a spring up in the hills. Animals were taken there to drink from the trough under the tap and everyone filled their clay pots with the water and carried them home for cooking, drinking and washing.

Olga was not used to these conditions and found life in the village so different to what she was used to. In addition to the hard conditions, Malamati picked on her continuously. Gianni had not realised that his young wife had to learn everything from housekeeping to farm work. He was patient and showed her how to pick fruit without bruising it. To pick strawberries he taught her to use her thumb and snip the fruit from the plant. He also showed her how to pick tobacco and corn. Lovingly he laughed at her mistakes, but Olga was not impressed. She felt humiliated and took it to heart.

Olga had a big load of clothes to wash and the river was flowing strongly. She placed the clothes in a pile by the river ready to wash. Suddenly Olga saw her mother-in-law's clothes, which had toppled over, floating down the river. She felt that she could not handle her mother-in-law any more and thought enough was enough. After three months of slavery, which felt like she had been there for years, she had had enough of married life, but she knew that if she went back to Malamati's home and stayed, she would be yelled at again.

Olga washed the remainder of the clothes then took them home and hung them on the line. While she was hanging the clothes she decided that she had had enough and could not take it anymore and she had to leave. She was not going to stay any longer. She packed her few belongings and put them into the sheet her parents had used for her when she got married and wondered where she would go. She was determined to leave that household.

#6

Olga Returns to Her Parents

Although Mama often laughed with my Giagia in later years about those clothes lost in the river, at the time it was no laughing matter.

The others were all in the fields. That was her opportunity to leave. She was not sure where she should go to, but she had no intention of staying at Malamati's place. She could go to Giannoula, her older sister, but she had her babies and was bringing up a young family. Olga did not want to be a burden to anyone. There was only one place she could go and that was to her parents' place. That was her home, so she walked to Florina.

After she walked for some time, the only sandals she owned fell apart. She pulled them off and continued along the dirt road in her bare feet. Olga was angry. She felt that she had been a failure as she had not settled into her husband's home. Married life was not for her. She would rather be out of it. She would much prefer to help her parents than toil for Malamati! It was not Gianni's house that she had just left, it was Malamati's! Gianni and Christopher worked from dawn to dusk in the fields and never complained. Malamati could do her own baking, washing and cleaning for her family from now on.

For the first time since she had married, Olga felt free. She knew that she should be happy in her life, not miserable. She loved her parents' home. It had a peaceful atmosphere where her Baba helped people in his chiropractic and naturopathic surgery. The home was only small, but it was clean and had some order. They were not rich and had few possessions, but they always had food on the table.

Her parents' home had a warm and friendly feel about it. Her Mama would start and end her day by standing in front of the iconostasi (icons), where she would pray and light a candle daily in one of the corners in their kitchen and cross herself and pray for her family. When they had their meals, her Baba always said grace and crossed himself. He always said that it was important to thank God for what they had. And while they ate there was laughter and enjoyment, while at Malamati's place there was no joy or laughter. Everyone was scared to say anything to Malamati in case they offended her.

Olga felt happy and skipped and walked and admired the scenery as she travelled home. Olga noticed the birds flying around as they dipped and glided, especially the little swallows that were catching insects. She felt so happy. People should have the right to be free and enjoy life as the little swallow did. She thought 'Oh! If only I could fly like the little swallow, fly and be free to enjoy God's creations'. Olga was enjoying her new-found freedom, the fresh air and the beautiful countryside. The spectacular colors of autumn were a reminder that nature was ready to go to sleep and reawaken in the spring.

Olga thought of Malamati's black clothes floating down the river. The clothes were free to travel down the river to far-off oceans. She laughed and laughed and it was the first time in months she had heard her own laughter. She felt so happy and carefree that she jogged with her load on her back down the road, stopping every now and then to pick some poppies, which were the last remnants of summer. God had created a beautiful place and she was determined to enjoy it from now on.

As she walked Olga wondered what Gianni would think. She could never tell with him, as he was not one to talk or express his thoughts. Her husband was not much of a talker, but when he did say something he had much wisdom and insight for a man who had never been to school. Her thoughts went to a man who was kind and gentle to the farm animals. She also remembered their first kiss. It was very gentle and soft. It was her first kiss and from what he told her it was his first kiss as well. Olga remembered their first night. She was terrified as she had never slept with a man before. She had taken her time to brush her hair then undressed and put her nightie on. The bedroom was lit as the moon shined through the window and she knew that Gianni was watching her every movement.

When she eventually climbed into the bed she found the mattress to be very rough and she could feel the straw sticking into her through the mattress cover. The discomfort caused her to mumble quietly.

"Olga, what is the matter?" Gianni asked gently. "The bed is so rough," replied Olga, "Things are sticking in to me."

"It's the straw. I filled the mattress with fresh straw as I thought it would be better than just the blankets on the bare boards. I know that some of the straw is sticking out." And he moved closer to her. With the moon shining through the window, Olga could see his strong manly face with his shining black eyes looking at her lovingly. He then gently caressed her body with a soft touch, the way she often saw him caress the animals.

"Do not be afraid," he murmured, "I will not hurt you. I am as nervous as you are. I have never touched a woman before. We will learn together." He drew her closer with his lips touching hers gently. Their kiss lingered for a long time then he rolled over saying, "We both have had a big day, little one. Relax. Go to sleep. Sweet dreams". Gianni's kisses and hugs were gentle and warm every night, but he never forced himself on her. He often said that there was plenty of time for them to get to know each other. Olga thought that for a hard-working man he was always gentle and kind. And Olga did enjoy having a brother, as Christopher was always there to help her. Olga had never known her brothers as they were all killed in the war before she was born.

As Olga approached her parents' home up the hill she wondered what they would say. Would they be angry with her? Had she failed them just as she had failed herself?

She found it very hard that she was returning to her parents, but she felt that she had no option. She knocked on the door. She knew it was midday and that her parents would be home. It was siesta time and in the towns they all rested, but not in the village of Tropaioukhos she had just left. In that village they worked all day long.

Sapfo, her younger sister, opened the door. She let out a squeal of excitement jumping up and down and yelling, "Mama, Baba, look who's here. Olga is here". Sapfo kissed and hugged her sister. Olga thought what a wonderful homecoming it was.

"Oh, my wonderful sister, Olga! Olga, it's so lovely to see you. Where's your handsome husband?" And Sapfo stuck her head out of the door looking for Gianni. "Gianni is not with me," replied Olga.

By then Anna, their younger sister, came running and the three sisters hugged and kissed each other and laughed in happiness. They were so happy to see one another again. The last time they had seen each other was three months ago at the wedding.

Zacharia and Olympia heard the squeals and laughter and came to see what was going on. "Olga, my child," Zacharia cried and hugged and kissed his daughter and held her tightly. "It is so good to see you. Where is your husband?"

"At home, Baba," Olga said quietly and lowered her head.

Zacharia looked at the bundle of clothes on the floor and then said "Are you staying a few days with us?"

"No! I'm staying for good, Baba, if you will have me," Olga said firmly.

"What?" Zacharia demanded. Olympia, his wife, came in and then hugged her daughter saying, "Welcome home, Olga. It's good to see you." She looked at her daughter's condition and saw that she had lost weight. Olga wore no shoes, but she was well tanned, obviously a result of working out in the fields.

"Come, my child, sit down and tell us how married life has been for you," Olga's Mama said.

"Sapfo, make us all a cup of mountain tea," Zacharia said. "Now tell us all about why you left your husband."

Olga began to cry and pleaded, "Baba, Mama, please do not make me go back to that house. My mother-in-law rules the household and all I get is abuse. She bosses me around. I cannot take it any more," Olga said.

Olympia reassured Olga, "My daughter, my mother-in-law yelled at me and even beat me, to teach me how to run the house. I was young like you and inexperienced like you."

"Mama, how can you say that? Do you mean that I have to be a slave to that household?" Olga said.

"More or less! Gradually you will have children and learn to run the household. Then the mother-in-law will sit by the fire nursing the young. She will be happy and content that you have given her grandchildren. She mellows with time as you learn to run the house. But mothers-in-law still like to keep on giving the orders all the time." Olympia tried to tell her daughter that most in-laws run the household with an iron fist. "Some are kind and rule with patience and care, but there are lots of in-laws who are very tough."

"Mama, I will not be a slave to Malamati any more. Please let me stay. I will do all the housework and will try to find work. I will not be a burden to you, I promise." Olga's tears rolled down her face as she pleaded with her parents.

Her Baba was concerned. "My child, did your husband beat you? You look so thin; you have lost a lot of weight."

"No... But, as I did not know how to work in the fields or housework, they all laughed at me. I did not know how to bake bread in the outside oven or light a fire or do the washing in the river." Then she burst out laughing as she again thought of Malamati's clothes floating down the river.

Zacharia was sad as he thought that possibly his daughter had lost the plot with her laughing. "My daughter, it's all right. This is your home, ena komati psome mazi tha to fame min stanahoriesser pethimou ("Fear not my child, with one piece of bread we shall all eat together").

Olga noticed that her Baba thought she had gone mad the way she laughed hysterically. "My dear Baba, I am not mad yet. I just remembered that while I was washing Malamati's clothes they all floated down the river and that was the last straw for me. I could not face her again. That was why I was laughing when I thought of her clothes floating down the river." Sapfo and Anna started laughing too. "I was not prepared to take any more abuse from her, but my life has not been a happy one. Gianni is kind and gentle, but he just takes the orders from his mother and gets on with his work. He has missed schooling, as he had to work from a very young age to support his mother and siblings, because his Baba had been taken away by the Ottoman authorities."

"Olga, your Mama and I want you to be happy, this is your home, and you're our daughter. We love you and we want you to stay. You are precious to us."

Olga slowly settled back home, helping her parents and sisters, and enjoying the caring and sharing of a loving family.

Over the next few months her Mama taught her the art of housekeeping. Olga treasured those months that she spent with her parents, although she kept thinking of Gianni, despite the fact that he did not come looking for her.

They laughed and enjoyed baking bread, buns and spanakopites (her Mama taught her the art of making filo pastry). Olympia taught Olga how to weave, sew, crochet and knit, how to light the fire and to cook and how to wash the clothes and then fold them neatly so that there were no creases. Gradually Olga started to enjoy housekeeping.

Olga would often help her mother at the bakery where her Mama worked, and was paid for the work she did. Olga saved her money so she could afford to buy material to make tablecloths, sheets and pillowcases and embroider linen. She bought material and crocheted curtains and doilies. She learnt to weave and make floor mats out of rags. She actually enjoyed the housework and loved helping her parents. Both her parents did not push her, but encouraged her to enjoy life and the art of housekeeping. They were smart in teaching her well enough to feel comfortable in handling a household.

Occasionally, Olga would make a comment such as, 'I wonder if Gianni would like that?'

On Thursdays, Sapfo was often sent to do the shopping in the local market after school. When she came home on one of those occasions Olga asked her sister, "Did you see Gianni, Sapfo?"

"No! There aren't many farmers around. There is a lot of talk that it will be a very long winter and they are busy storing and preserving their fruit and vegetables in their cellars," Sapfo replied.

Olga realised by then that she should be with her husband helping him. In mid November Sapfo came back from the markets very excited. "Olga, I saw Gianni and he gave me all this fruit and vegetables. He said that I didn't have to pay for it. He said it was for you."

Olga was feeling guilty as she thought that he needed to sell all the produce in order to buy the few necessities such as matches, soap, salt, sugar and oil. Sapfo looked at her sister excitedly and said, "He asked how you were, and if you're happy".

"And what did you tell him, Sapfo?" Olga asked.

"I told him the truth that you are very happy at home and that other men have sent proxies for your hand. And that you will never, never go back because Malamati yells at you and they all laughed at you."

"Sapfo, you and your big mouth! You didn't?" Olga yelled at her sister.

"Well it is true. Baba is getting people coming asking if you are free to marry," Sapfo said.

"I know, but others do not have to know what is going on in our home," Olga said. Olga knew that other young men kept on sending proxy representatives to enquire if she was available. Olga knew it was not right as she was already married, but she was honoured to be acknowledged by others. She also knew that divorce was out of the question as people and the Church frowned upon it. Besides, Olga often thought she would rather stay single and be content.

"Gianni said that he knew you were not happy as you never laughed or smiled. You were always angry and often cried. He does not want you to be sad. He said that you have a beautiful face and when you get annoyed your green eyes shine. He also said that he and his brother missed the bread you baked and loved to come home to see you brighten the house with the flowers that were in the clay pot. You brightened the place up. He misses all that. He misses you, but he wants you to be happy," Sapfo said.

"He said that?" Olga asked quietly.

"I told him that you will never go back as you are very happy at home helping Mama and Baba."

"Oh Sapfo, you didn't say that?" Olga could not believe what her sister Sapfo was telling her.

"Yes I did. I told him the truth," replied Sapfo.

"What did Gianni say to that?" asked Olga.

"Oh! He chuckled and said that he would see. And by the way, I still think he is tall, dark and handsome," Sapfo said, and then grabbed one of the juicy apples and raced out the back to tell her parents that they had some lovely fresh fruit and vegetables, which they often could not afford.

For Olga, the days dragged into weeks and then into months. Eventually Christmas was upon them and the snow was heavy that year. Zacharia cut a branch from a pine and placed it in one of the corners of the room as the girls wrapped walnuts in cellophane and hung them on the tree with some white cotton wool. Olympia put the cross on top of the tree. The girls made a lovely nativity scene with sticks and rags. They sang Christmas carols together. When village children came to the door singing Christmas carols Olympia always had some little goodies for each one of them to put in their bags.

Olga wondered what Gianni was doing for Christmas, putting her head down as she went on with her embroidery. Olga had mixed feelings. Had she been too immature at the time to leave her husband? Was her decision to leave too rushed? There were others in similar situations, but they stuck it out. She was very angry with herself, missing the opportunity of going to college and the way the wedding was rushed. Although there had been little time for her to really think about it all, Olga spent winter reflecting on her life.

Throughout the winter Zacharia and his family all worked inside their home because of the cold and snow. Zacharia sorted out his different ointments and herbs, mixing various mixtures on the old combustion stove. The girls helped if they could. They also helped their mother with sewing, knitting or crocheting.

Sapfo and Anna attended the local school. Olga often helped them with their schoolwork. Sapfo was determined that she was going to be a nurse so she only needed to go to mid-year high school and then she hoped to go to Thessaloniki to do her training.

By March the snows were melting and spring was in the air. Olga often walked over the mountains with her Baba, helping him pick the wild herbs. She enjoyed the smell of the spring blossoms and the new growth of thyme, sage and lavender growing in the wild, and the red poppies springing up in the fields. The swallows had returned to build their nests, a sign that life continues. It was during this time that Olga wondered if she belonged somewhere else.

Zacharia watched his daughter. He was very proud of her. Would Gianni come for her? Had he been too quick to marry her off to the first proxy that came around? He only wanted the best for his daughters. He was getting old and losing all his six sons in the World War I was the hardest thing for his wife and himself. He had wanted to pass his trade on to his sons, but they were all dead. How could he pass on the trade that had been passed from Baba to son for generations? Could he change and pass on all his secrets to his daughters? Should he just start teaching Olga his trade? Would people trust a woman? These questions plagued him, but he decided that it might be the best thing he could do for her since he was the cause of her unhappiness.

There were other male suitors approaching him for Olga's hand, but Zacharia did not want to tell them that his daughter was already married. Could she get a divorce? What would people say? She was starting to gain some weight again and her round face with the bright green eyes and flowing auburn hair was attracting young men. Zacharia started to get Olga to help him more and more with his patients. She was good with people and very gentle with the suction cups and in massaging people. She was terrified of milking the snakes for their venom. She would not have a bar of that, but she was fine with the leeches, although she only helped because her Baba asked her to assist him. She was good in helping to put a child's arm in splints, but she was not able to prepare the little splints in the same way that her Baba made them. Zacharia knew he must teach her so Olga would have a trade.

Zacharia wanted more than anything else in the world for Olga to be happy. He was sure that, with his wife's guidance and encouragement, Olga was now better equipped to be a wife. Olympia and Zacharia prayed every night that God would help their daughters to find happiness. They came to realise that times had changed and that they had been too zealous in forcing Olga to marry at such a young age.

It was now the 15th of March and Olga was now 15 years old. She had been back home since early September. In those six months Olga had not heard from Gianni. She often wondered if she had overreacted and whether or not she should go back to him. But could she face her mother-in-law? Olga felt that she really didn't belong in her parents' home and she should be with her husband. Olga was beginning to think like an adult.

#7

GIANNI COMES FOR OLGA

Olga began to enjoy helping her *Baba* with his patients. And she often helped people who had bad backs. They used glass suction cups (*vandouzes*) to ease the pain. She had a long forklike instrument wrapped in cotton wool, which she would then dip into the menthylated spirits liquid her *Baba* had prepared. She would light it, insert it in the cup and then pull the lit cotton out in order to create the suction and quickly place the cup on the patient's back or wherever there was pain. She had to be very careful as the flame was burning all the time until the actual procedure was finished. She had to massage each patient with healing oils after the suction-cup application.

While Olga was doing this her *Baba* was busy preparing the various creams and ointments for his patients to take home. Her *Baba* trusted Olga as he taught her the different techniques more and more with his various patients.

One afternoon the rest of the family was having their afternoon naps while Olga was working on embroidering a tablecloth. (This siesta time was quite common in Greece and still is today.) Her thoughts were of *'what should she do? Should she go back to her husband? Should she give her marriage another chance?'* Olga was in turmoil. She could not decide if she should just wipe that disaster out of her life and take another direction. She knew that there was another young man who was showing particular interest in her. Was that the way to go?

An acquaintance from college had approached her; he had been a year ahead of her at college. He met Olga again as she was heading home after helping her *Mama* at the bakery. He was a young man who also could not finish his schooling as his parents could not afford to send him to the college when it had been relocated to the other town. So now he was training as a carpenter's apprentice. When Olga explained to him that she was married but had left her husband as things had not worked out he told her that he was very interested in her and was prepared to wait for her if she was to get a divorce. He was very outgoing as he had a high opinion of himself. He said that he was quite happy for her to take her time so that he could finish his apprenticeship before they were married. But she was not impressed with the way he came up to her taking everything for granted and was so open about things. While she thought that he seemed a nice enough person, he should have approached her *Baba* first as she still respected her parents and their traditions. Olga's mind was in turmoil wondering which course to take. She was saying a little prayer as she concentrated on embroidering the tablecloth, '*Please Lord, help me and guide me. I need you to lead the way. Which road do I take?*'

Suddenly she heard a knock at the front door. She put the tablecloth down and opened the door. It was Gianni. "Gianni! Gianni! What are you doing here?" Olga asked excitedly.

"I have come to talk to you and your parents. Can I come in?"

"Yes... Yes. Come in and I will find them." Olga quickly called out to her parents.

"*Mama*, *Baba*! Gianni is here." They all hurried into the living room.

Gianni was standing, looking out of the window and thinking to himself, *'What a fool I am! What am I doing here? I know that Olga is beautiful! But she is so young.What is wrong with me?'*

The three walked in. "Gianni, Gianni, it is so good to see you, my son." Zacharia hugged and kissed Gianni on both cheeks and then said "Please sit down. Tell us how you have been. Olga, please bring us some refreshments. Tsai, raki? What would you like?"

"A drink of water please," Gianni responded. "I am fine. It has been a very long winter, but spring is here. There is a lot of work to be done in preparing the fields and planting the crops, but it will be a good year. Already the goats have had their kids, the sow has had her piglets and the cow has had a calf. It has been a good start for spring. I am sure that this season will be a prosperous one." He swallowed hard, took a deep breath then continued awkwardly, "I... know Olga is young, but she is my wife and I want her back."

"Gianni, Olga is young. It was my mistake. Times have changed. My wife was 14 when we got married. That was a long time ago and it is not the same any more. It was wrong for me to agree to this marriage. Forgive me, my son. I only want her happiness. Olga, you do not want to go back, do you?" Zacharia said.

Olga stared at her *Baba*. She felt sorry for him because he only wanted the best for his daughters, as she well knew. He was not well and he seemed to have aged more lately. When he was walking up the mountain collecting the various herbs, he would often stop and sit as he was out of breath. Her mouth opened and closed as she struggled for words, looking at Gianni. He did look handsome just as her younger sister Sapfo had said. He was tall, had shining, black, wavy hair and dark-brown eyes. She then thought of all the past tears and exclaimed "I will not return, Gianni. You yell and laugh at me because I do not know how to work in the fields and I have to do all the housework".

"Olga, Olga... I did not mean to hurt you; I just wanted you to learn. I had not realised that you were only 14. You look older and I thought you were possibly 17 or 18. You walk and talk so maturely for your age. I know I laughed at you, but it was not to hurt you. You just looked so funny when you were working so awkwardly out in the field. I have missed you. I miss your cooking, the clean house and the clean clothes, even though you have lost a few of the clothes in the river!" and he grinned. "And your fresh bread was so delicious.

"Actually, we all miss you. Christopher has gone back to baking our bread and he is not that impressed. As you well know our mother is no housekeeper nor is she a good cook. I know you are young, but you were doing a great job. And by the way, I have been able to get a wash tub for you so that you do not have to go down to the river and lose any more clothes," Gianni said, again with a grin on his face.

"You did? And you missed me?" said a surprised Olga.

Olympia and Zacharia looked at each other. They felt that there was a little spark of love in both of them. Zacharia turned to his daughter and said, "Olga, your husband is a hard-working man. He has a good heart. It was unfortunate that we had rushed things originally, but I believe he will look after you. Gianni, if you can show patience and understanding with Olga, as she had not done that work before, I am sure that in time she will learn".

"Olga, you did look so funny trying to light the fire as often all the ash blew on to your face. And when you worked in the fields, you kept pulling out more plants than the weeds, and as for picking the fruit, you broke many branches when picking the fruit," said Gianni, laughing.

"There he goes again. He is laughing at me. How can I go back?" Olga cried out.

Zacharia looked at them both and said, "My *Baba* had told me these words as your *Mama* and I too had lots of misunderstandings and arguments. Learn to communicate with each other in order for a marriage to work. Give and take. Like a rose bush, you trim it and it blooms. So it is with marriage. You must have *Agape* (God's love}, *Erota* (physical love) and *Phillia* (friendship love). Combining the three loves is not easy. You have to work hard at helping each other. Be patient with each other. Each one of you has something to offer the other. Encourage each other. Forgive, forget, laugh with each other and love each other.

Trust God in all things. You must walk with the light, Jesus' light. These words must always be in your heart. *Oh Christos Nika Ta Panda* (Christ conquers all). Learn to pray together and trust in God. Do not be afraid. Jesus' light will shine on your path. Life will have its ups and downs. You need the rain to fully appreciate the sunshine in your lives. *H Dunami Tou Theou na ine Pandode mazi sas* (May God's strength be always with you)."

Gianni reflected on the time his *Baba* held him for just a few minutes in the barn and blessed him, and said "God's strength to be with you".

Olympia spoke gently, "Gianni, do you feel that you can take care of my daughter, to love, care and respect her?"

"Yes! I will do my best to look after her," Gianni said.

Zacharia turned to his daughter and asked, "Olga, will you go back to your husband, respect him, care for him and love him?" He stopped and looked closely at his daughter. "You must be very sure as life is not easy."

Olga was so tense. She looked at Gianni and then at her parents. They all remained silent. While Zacharia and Olympia waited for Olga's answer they could hear the birds chirping outside. No-one made a sound. Gianni looked at Olga anxiously. He wanted to shout *'I need you. I want you beside me. You are the light of my heart. I can't understand it, but you are in my thoughts day and night. You are in my soul, you are in my heart'*, but he didn't. He just waited patiently for an answer.

The more time Olga took to answer, the more impatient Gianni became. He wanted to yell at her, *'For goodness sake woman, say yes!'* But he still remained silent. He wanted Olga's answer to come from her heart.

Olga thought God had opened doors for her as she had been praying before she had heard the knock on the door. In a quiet tone Olga replied, "Yes, I belong with my husband". Gianni was so excited. He jumped up, hugged Olga, and then hugged both his mother-in-law and his father-in-law. Turning to Olga he then said, "Let's go home, my *koukla mou* (doll)".

#8

Olga returns to Tropaioukhos

Over the years my parents often talked about their trials and tribulations, and certainly their life was not an easy one. Their strong faith, especially *Mama's* prayers, which she said daily as she stood in front of her *iconostasi* (the icons of Jesus, St Nikolaos and St George and other saints), held them together. She thanked God and prayed for the safety of all her loved ones. *Pray without ceasing (1 Thess 5-17).* My parents both felt the strong presence of Jesus in their lives.

Gianni and Olga farewelled her family and headed for their home on foot, a journey that took over an hour. They were strangers to each other (they had only known each other for three months) and it was not easy for them, heading back to Malamati's house once again. They were bound by tradition. They were married, but not knowing each other was a challenge for both of them. Although they were young and inexperienced in life, they both knew in their hearts they had to try to make the marriage work. Olga felt that God was certainly there to help them as she had just finished praying when Gianni had knocked at the door. She was certain that God had answered her prayer and told her which road to take.

Gianni walked fast and Olga, carrying her belongings, tried to keep up, but her load was heavy. She had all the lovely handiwork she had made. She wanted to yell at Gianni, *'For goodness sake, Gianni, help me!'* But she was stubborn and so was he. The problem with both of them was that they were two headstrong, determined people who would not give in to the other.

Although Gianni was happy that Olga was returning with him he was also annoyed. He remembered his mother's words *'You are bowing to a woman if you go there for her'*. He did not know what was wrong with him. He just followed his instincts. Gianni was attracted to Olga from the start and he could not understand himself. He had never been attracted to any other woman as he was to Olga. He knew he had to follow his gut feelings and pray that things would work out for them. Gianni knew he was bound to Olga, as she was his wife even though she was very young. He had to try to make their relationship work. He had to persevere. He felt that God's light was guiding him and he was thrilled when Zacharia blessed them with the words *H Dunami Tou Theou na ine Pandode mazi sas* (May God's strength be always with you). This was the same blessing his *Baba* had given him. He felt so inspired, so pleased, as he walked quickly thinking about these things. Although Gianni was in the lead he was sure that Jesus was leading the way.

After almost an hour Olga had had enough and sat down on the side of the road. She was angry with Gianni. *'What's wrong with the man? He was all sweet and loving at my parents' place, but look at him now,'* she thought. Gianni was at least 100 metres ahead of her and he didn't seem to want to know her.

Suddenly Gianni realised that Olga was not walking beside him. He looked back and saw her sitting on the side of the road. *'What is wrong with the woman?'* he thought to himself, his anger rising. He walked back to her and yelled, "Are you coming? I have a lot of work to do!"

"No! You go ahead. You can go!" Olga yelled back.

Trying to be calm he asked, "What's wrong?"

"This bundle is so heavy and I am tired. Could we catch the bus?" Olga replied.

"No! Everyone will talk!" Gianni said loudly. He wondered why he said that, as he really didn't care what others thought or said. Gianni liked his own company.

"I don't care what people say. I have done nothing wrong," Olga said loudly.

"You have done nothing wrong?" Gianni yelled. "You have humiliated me!" (He wondered why was he was saying things like that, but then he was embarrassed when his wife left him.) "You are the only wife in the village who has gone back to her parents. You are my wife, for better or for worse! You are mine, and don't forget it!"

That was the first time Olga had seen him angry. '*So he has got some guts in him,*' Olga thought. She looked at him, saw his dark eyes shining and said quietly "I am sorry. I didn't mean to hurt you. It was your mother who drove me away. I could not stand her yelling and screaming and ordering me around. And I am wondering if I am doing the right thing in coming back".

Gianni moved closer to Olga and said calmly, "Come, give me the load that you are carrying and we will face her together. We will carry the load together". They did not realise what lay ahead of them, but certainly they knew that the road was not going to be an easy one for them. Gianni lifted the bundle as if it was a bundle of feathers and started walking; ensuring that this time they walked side-by-side. He remembered a saying someone had related to him. *'If a marriage is to succeed, you must walk side by side, not one in front and the other following.'*

Arriving at the old house Olga was nervous. Thankfully Malamati and Christopher were in the fields and that gave them a little time together. Gianni took the bundle into their bedroom and threw it on to the bed. Olga followed him and noticed that an old cupboard had been put in the bedroom. On the bed she saw that a lovely soft doona and two new pillows had been placed there. Olga touched them and she said, "They're lovely, they are so soft!"

"I saved all the feathers from the chickens and had the seamstress make a mattress, doona and pillows for you. It should be a lot more comfortable than the straw mattress, " Gianni said.

He was so proud of that achievement. Olga said that she had found out later on that he had actually gone around to the relatives, friends and neighbours, collecting all their feathers to make that mattress and doona.

"Gianni, this is beautiful," said Olga as she sat on the bed.

Olga was so pleased that she had not been the only one who had been working all winter. She then opened the bundle and showed Gianni what he had been carrying – handmade embroidered tablecloths and sheets, and the pillowcases and rugs that she had made.

"They are lovely," he exclaimed. "Well it seems that both of us have been busy during winter. Come and I will show you a few more surprises."

Olga followed Gianni to the cellar. He had made her a *scarffy* – a wash tub and scrubbing board. "I know how much you loved going to the river to do the washing," he chuckled.

In the kitchen he had built a few shelves and also a tub for Olga to knead the dough to make bread. He was very proud of his work. They were not much, but they certainly made life a little easier for Olga.

"Gianni, all winter I felt that I belonged with my husband," Olga quietly admitted.

"Olga, you know that it will not be easy. Until we build our own home, we have to live with my mother. You know that we have to be patient." Gianni came closer to her as he said that.

"I know," Olga whispered.

"Promise me that you will never, never leave me. I need you..." Gianni said as he held Olga in his arms and kissed her tenderly.

Olga and Gianni worked hard all afternoon. She cleaned the house while he cleaned and fed the animals. Olga cleaned the windows and put up the crocheted curtains she had made. She then washed the floors with warm water and kerosene and then put down the new rugs. When this was done she polished the old table and placed the tablecloth on it and put a pottery vase in the centre. Gianni interrupted his work with the animals to bring in some cherry blossoms and put them in the vase. He knew that Olga loved flowers.

"They are beautiful! Thank you, Gianni," Olga said as she admired the spring blossoms.

Gianni also cleaned the old slow combustion stove, stocked it with fresh firewood and then lit it. Olga made some lentil soup and put it on the stove. She then kneaded some dough to make bread, while Gianni lit the fire in the brick oven that was out in the yard to bake the bread. Together they worked in the hope that this would please Malamati.

Gianni went back to finish cleaning the stables and fetching the animals from the yards. Malamati and Christopher came home to find a clean, fresh house. The aromas were flowing through the house with the fresh bread and a large salad spread on the table and the lentil soup simmering away on the stove. Christopher said, "The house looks beautiful and the food smells wonderful. It is good to see you home. We missed your cooking and you".

"Thank you, Christopher," Olga said.

Malamati glared at Christopher and then said to Olga, "I have been working all day. I am hungry". (Olga knew that she would be tested so she actually said a little prayer and remembered the words from the Bible, *Blessed is the man who perseveres.)* The Greek tradition was that when a woman married, her husband's parents became her parents. She had to respect them no matter what. It was not easy for many young married couples as in-laws ruled with iron fists.

Olga said, "Sit down, *Mama,* and I will serve dinner in a little while. I have brought you all presents. I will get them" and she went into her bedroom and returned with the gifts that she had made for all of them. Olga had knitted Malamati a black cardigan and had bought her a pair of slippers. She handed them to Malamati and then kissed her hand as a sign of respect, just as Gianni was walking into the living room. He broke the silence saying, "The food smells great, and I am hungry".

"Sit down and I will serve the soup, Gianni," Olga replied.

But before she served the soup Olga handed Christopher his presents, a pair of slippers and a new shirt. She then gave Gianni a pair of slippers to put on. Olga had an ulterior motive in giving them all slippers. She wanted to teach them to leave their shoes in the cellar before they all came up the stairs so that this would ensure that house would be kept clean. They did that at her parents' home. She was hoping she could teach them to do the same if they had slippers. This would keep the floor free from the mud and dirt and save her time cleaning.

Christopher was thrilled. "I have never worn slippers. I always go barefoot inside when I take off my boots."

Gianni said firmly, "It is good to have slippers; it will keep your feet warm and the house clean," as he smiled at his wife. He knew that Olga was trying to educate his family.

Malamati was happy for her son. He was smiling for a change. But she wondered how Olga, a young city girl, would be able to cope with the rough lifestyle and the hard work of country life. Malamati thought that at least Olga had the courage to come back and try again. However, Olga was certainly not going to get any sympathy from Malamati. Olga would have to swim or sink. She was young and very much alive, but Malamati knew that when working day and night in the harsh land of the mountains, people became old before their time. Malamati was possibly in her late 40s, (she did not know her exact age), but felt like an old woman.

Malamati resented Olga strongly, and Olga could not understand the reason for this. Was it because of her youth, looks or spirit, or was it that she had taken her son's love? Whatever the reason, at every opportunity she had Malamati would denigrate Olga in front of her sons and others.

Olga and Gianni were married so that they could obtain a block of land to farm and build their home, but they still had to pay the Government. They could not believe this, as they were supposed to have been given the land as compensation for losing all the property in Turkey. But no! The Government still demanded that they pay for it over a period of years. Nevertheless, Olga and Gianni were happy as the block of land was in the centre of town and was situated across from the school. Malamati's house was across the road from them. *Thea* Mersina's place was opposite and the spring water tap, which flowed continually, was beside the land.

The family all worked very hard together, planting and harvesting the beans, onions, corn, potatoes, tobacco, strawberries, cucumbers and grapes. The tobacco had been sold for a very good price that year, so with the money they had saved they felt there would be enough to start building their home.

The spring water tap was always overflowing from the trough. The villagers all came and filled their water jugs from the tap and the animals were watered from the trough. Gianni had diverted the water that overflowed from the trough to his land in order to water all the fruit trees he had planted. When Gianni had planted all the fruit trees, he had no idea that the fruit would supplement their diet in the years to come. The trees flourished with the water that was irrigated on to the property. There were apricots, plums, cherries, apples, quince, pears and a mulberry tree. Gianni built a chicken house and fenced the yard to keep their chickens from wandering away.

Gianni and Olga worked hard and whenever they had time they would travel up and down the river collecting the large rocks to build a cellar. Gianni started building his cellar hoping to build the house on top of the cellar. In the mountains the villagers needed their cellars to store all their food and to house their animals during the bleak winters. Usually the cellar was dug, then lined with the rocks and slate collected from the riverbeds.

Whenever the village had Saints' Day celebration or some other festive occasion Gianni and Olga would stop working in the fields, but would continue to construct their home.

Occasionally Olga attended the village celebrations if there were dances, but Gianni would not attend as he had never learnt to dance and was embarrassed to try. Olga and Christopher would go and enjoy the dances and the festivities. Olga was pleased to have a brother-in-law, especially when he escorted her. And they both enjoyed the odd occasions to dance and celebrate with all the other villagers.

#9
Life in Tropaioukhos

Life in Tropaioukhos continued with the usual routine. Olga kept house and worked beside Gianni planting and harvesting and saving enough to build their own home so that they could move out of Malamati's house. Olga was always careful not to upset her because she was the one who ruled the roost. Married life was not easy, but Olga came to know the other young people in the village and she found out that they were all in, more or less, a similar situation. In some households fathers-in-law ruled, while in others, like hers, it was the mothers-in-law.

Olga wanted her friend Paraskevoulla, who was a similar age to Olga, to marry her brother-in-law Christopher, but unfortunately it never eventuated as she was married off to a young man by proxy in another village. They had common interests and helped each other with their weaving, knitting and their farm work. She missed her friend when she left the village.

Olga also enjoyed *Thea* Mersini's company. They lived next-door so it was good to have someone to talk to. She was Malamati's sister-in-law and *Thea* also had her mother-in-law to look after so she knew what it was like. She had a tribe of kids and she worked hard to feed them. Her husband, Parashos Deliyannis, who was educated, liked to spend time in the *cafenio* (coffee shop) to argue politics or to read his paper and give orders, while *Thea* Mersini worked day and night to feed and clothe the family. When he felt that he should go and plough fields he would, but generally it was *Thea* Mersini who worked hard. Life for her was very difficult, but she was a proud mother and wife.

Work commenced early in the day in the village. At the crack of dawn all the families would load the tools on to their carts and then head for their various plots of land. Many of the plots were next to each other so they would help each other hoeing, planting and harvesting. It was not unusual for women to work until the last day of their pregnancy before giving birth.

Olga and Gianni's *koubarri* (best man) and his pregnant wife both worked in the fields until she went into labour. She squatted and had the baby while her husband picked up the baby and tied the umbilical cord. Then she put the baby on her back and continued working. When the baby needed to be fed, if they had a shady tree to sit under they found that a luxury. She breastfed the baby and then went back to picking, planting or harvesting. Olga was intrigued that these women did not moan or groan, they just got on with life. They were always thankful for their daily bread as they worked very hard to simply feed and clothe their families.

Life was very simple with no modern facilities. Their light at night was by an oil lamp, and the water was carted from the only spring water communal tap in the centre of the village. The women worked hard all day helping the men in the fields and then during the night they weaved rugs or sewed and knitted their clothes with the aid of their oil lamp.

At night when the families had to thread the tobacco leaves, they all sat in someone's yard sharing jokes and stories while they threaded the leaves. They all sat around in a circle with the fire in the middle to shed light and to keep them warm as they all worked hard cleaning corn or threading tobacco. The tobacco leaves were threaded together and hung on timber frames to dry. When they cleaned corn they would laugh and joke as they worked together. Their lives were difficult, but they all upheld, shared and cared for each other.

Life was not all rosy. There were fights at times. For example, if one person had taken more water from the irrigation channel or encroached on another's land they would not talk to each other for a while. But life went on. Saints' Days were times of special celebrations and the villagers would all celebrate in the village centre. They'd dance and kick up their heels and shake hands again. If for any reason some were stubborn and did not mix, they all felt that he (or she) was simply a stubborn mule.

As time passed fights and arguments would be forgotten and life continued in the same routine. They all knew each other and had a common interest to survive and provide for their family.

#10
Gianni's and Olga's Son

Olga was still a teenager when she fell pregnant. She was just 15 years old. She would climb trees to pick fruit and worked day and night helping in the fields as well as keeping house for Gianni, Malamati and Christopher. Her life was not an easy one, but she put her trust in God daily. And with Jesus' strength she made the best of each day. She was not the only one with problems. She found there were others in the village who also had similar difficulties. She made many friends, which meant that they had each others' shoulders to cry or laugh on.

She gave birth to a healthy son on the 15th of October, 1934. Both Olga and Gianni were very proud parents.

As was the Greek tradition, Gianni and Olga were going to name their son Athanasis after Gianni's father and had discussed this with the godfather, Eustratios Koutsoubithis. But unfortunately the godfather had other ideas. When the priest was baptising the baby, he said to the godfather "and what is the child's name?"

The godfather proudly announced "*Heraklis* (Hercules), after the mighty *Heraklis*", as he loved ancient history.

Gianni and Olga were stunned, and they complained and argued "You cannot name our son that!"

The arguments continued and the priest nearly threw all of them out of the church.

"Yes, I can. I am the godfather and that's our tradition. The godfather names the child. I am your *koubarri* and now your child's *nounos* (godfather). Have some respect for me."

They were very disappointed with the naming of the child, but they loved their son and hoped that when they had another child it would have the grandfather's name.

Like all the other women in the village, Olga took the baby into the fields with her. When the baby cried she stopped working, hoping to find a tree to sit under, fed him and then continued working. If there was no tree nearby, she would sit in the open ground.

Whenever possible, Olga would visit her parents in Florina, so that her parents could enjoy their grandson. They loved their grandson and were very proud of him. And Malamati started to mellow a little now that she had a grandson to brag about.

The small house was becoming crowded and Olga and Gianni worked hard to finish their home. All the fruit trees were thriving and bearing fruit, which gave them another income. Olga was proud of Gianni as he loved his family and would always be working and trying to improve their lifestyle.

Gianni would go up into the mountains, cut timber and bring it back in a cart to build a chicken pen. Then he fenced a yard and bought some chickens. Olga was proud of his hard work, especially when they started getting eggs every day, and were even able to sell some. But one night all the chickens were killed or taken by foxes. Gianni and Olga were devastated, annoyed and angry in losing the chickens because they had worked so hard to house and raise the hens. To lose all of them in one night was a disaster. So they started again and Gianni had to make sure that the fence was strong and the foxes were not able to steal any more chickens.

#11
GIANNI'S AND OLGA'S SECOND SON IS BORN

Four years later Gianni's and Olga's second son was born on the 20th of April, 1938. They were very happy, even though Olga was hoping for a girl. But she was happy to see a healthy son. Once again Gianni was thrilled and very proud.

When the time came for their son to be baptised they visited their *koubarri* who were to be the godparents. To be certain that there would be no surprises they asked if they would name the child after Gianni's father, Athanasis. It was all agreed and Gianni and Olga were happy that it was all settled beforehand. Surely they would not have any argument with the godfather this time.

Gianni and Olga handed over the baby and as the priest said "The child is to be named..." and looked to the godfather.

The godfather stood close to the priest looking at all the people and then said very loudly "The child is to be name after Eleftherios Venizelos, the Prime Minister who had founded modern Greece".

The priest looked at the godfather and then at the parents. He had understood that the naming had been settled and that the baby was to be named Athanasis. He was not impressed when the godfather spoke.

An argument broke out again between the parents and the godfather. They were angry and ready to walk out of the church. But where would they go? It cost money to go to the city to baptise a child. The priest repeated angrily, "What is the name this child is to be called? If you cannot agree you will all have to leave the church".

The parents called out "Athanasis, after the child's grandfather".

"No! No! I am the godfather. The child should be named after our Prime Minister. He was a hero to this country and we must honour him. The child is to be called Eleftherios Venizelos. That is it".

The priest responded, "No, the child can only have one name, it will be Eleftherios and that is all. No arguments from all of you, do you hear? This baptism has turned into a debacle. This is a sacred place, have some respect".

Once again Gianni and Olga were devastated, asking themselves "How can this be?" They went home very annoyed and even though they had respected their Greek traditions they were upset with the godfather.

They also knew that the priest and the godfather often shared coffee at the *cafenio* so even if they argued the parents felt that they could not have changed anything.

Olga and Gianni continued to work hard as the house had to be finished. They now had the two boys to feed and it was becoming crowded in Malamati's home.

Olga often prayed: "*Please Lord Jesus, all I would like for my family is a roof over our heads even if it's only one room. At least all the family would be together in their own home and not have to rely on Malamati for their accommodation.*"

As Heraklis and Eleftherios were growing up they would get into mischief and annoy Malamati and then arguments would often break out. At times it was unbearable and uncomfortable for all of them. Gianni finished the cellar dividing it into two rooms, one for the animals and another for their cellar to store all their food. He was hoping to start building the house upstairs soon.

#12
GIANNI GOES TO WAR

World War II had commenced.

On 28th of October, 1940, Mussolini's Italian Government demanded that the Greek Prime Minister allow the Italian and the German armies to march through Greece. Prime Minister Metaxas refused with a single word, *'OCHI!'* (No!). This solitary word became a Greek battle cry.

But Mussolini did not wait. The soldiers began moving across the border from Albania into Greece, and Greece was exposed to World War II. Greece's entry into the war was forced on to it by that invasion.

Gianni left Olga behind with Heraklis, who was six years old and Eleftherios who was two. Gianni's platoon was issued with horses so that they could ride through the rough terrain of the mountain passes. Olga watched Gianni leave. He was riding his horse and looked so proud in his uniform. Olga held Eletfherios in her arms and Heraklis tugged at her skirt while they waved to Gianni and the rest of the platoon. Her tears rolled down her cheeks as she prayed, *"Please God, look after my man, and bring him back safe and well. My children need their father"*.

Gianni and Christopher were conscripted into the army together with all other eligible males in the village. Conscription applied throughout Greece. The platoon Gianni was in was sent to the Albanian border in an attempt to stop the Italians moving into Greece. Despite Italian superiority in numbers and equipment, determined Greek defenders drove the invaders back into Albania.

#13
WORLD WAR II REACHES GREECE

The Italian army first came through the villages up in the highlands, leaving death and destruction in their path.

When the Greek Army drove the Italians back into Albania early in 1941, Hitler was forced to defend his southern flank by diverting German troops to attack Greece. By the end of May 1941 the Germans had overrun the whole of the country, although Greek resistance was never entirely suppressed.

Malamati and Olga had to survive, so they still worked from dawn to dusk in their fields. The two boys helped their mother all the time. Olga had taught them both to help her in the fields, even though they were both very young. Heraklis was a hard-working young man for six years old. He followed his *Mama's* instructions; as she made the holes for the seedlings he followed her and he would put the seedlings in the holes.

He worked hard alongside his *Mama* planting, digging and harvesting, and helping his younger brother. And Eleftherios, even though he was a toddler, had to help and do all his chores such as feeding the chooks or pulling out the rocks or roots as his brother or *Mama* ploughed. He followed behind sorting out all the roots for the fire or the rocks for the fencing of the borders of the fields.

Olga could never please her mother-in-law even though the boys and she were always working in the farm. She often wondered whether she should go back to her parents with her boys as life could be better for them. But she had promised Gianni that she would never leave him. This was his home and her children's home.

Olga, Malamati and the boys were working in the fields when the postman delivered THAT telegram. The telegram stated that Gianni had been lost in the war. It said that although his body had not been recovered, his entire platoon had been killed in action when fighting the Italians on the Albanian border.

When Olga read the telegram she fell on her knees crying. "*Ochi! Ochi!* (No! No!) It cannot be possible." Malamati grabbed the telegram and read it. She started screaming, "First my husband was lost in the War, then my only daughter Despina, now my eldest son. *Ochi!*"

Both women were screaming, crying and pulling their hair in anguish. The two little boys held their mother tightly, puzzled at what had happened.

The battles continued to rage fiercely throughout Greece with more patriots either killed or wounded.

Christopher was released from the Army as he had no father and his elder brother (Gianni) had been lost in action. This was a common occurrence to enable men to look after their families. But it did not take long for Christopher to meet a lovely lady (Ourania) from a neighbouring village and get married. Ourania settled in with the family, but Malamati's house was very crowded by now.

Olga, now dressed in black, battled on to survive with her two little boys. Everyone in the village was struggling from the invasion and from lack of food. It was not easy to work in the fields with war raging on, and especially when landmines had been planted by both armies. Many people lost their lives when they tried to work in the fields. Olga often said that they were still very thankful to have a crust of bread and a tomato or onion to fill their stomachs. Many people in the city were starving as the enemy had stopped all their food supplies. Athens, the capital, was hit the hardest. Children and the elderly were dying of starvation. In the winter of 1941-42 more then 300,000 people starved to death.

The people from the towns and cities walked for miles scavenging for food from the side of the roads and open fields, picking bitter herbs or greens to eat. Many died doing this. The rich sent servants to the villages to buy bread, which often cost a fortune. Cats or rats were eaten when rabbits could not be found. As every sparrow or bird of any kind was found they were killed and eaten. Barley was ground and used as a substitute for coffee. Corn was ground to make bread or porridge and caused the swelling of undernourished stomachs. Olga had never seen so many people begging for a crust of bread.

Olga's two sisters, Sapfo and Anna, often came from Florina to help her by working in the fields. In return Olga supplied them with fruit and vegetables. Olga was so thankful that Gianni had planted all the fruit trees as they were a great supplement to their diet. She would dry the apricots, quinces, apples and pears; all the fruit came in very handy.

The Germans were now marching down to their village. The Italians had already been through pillaging, burning and destroying houses and killing anyone in their path. The villagers dreaded the prospect of the Germans coming too. They had heard the stories of the Germans raping inhabitants, and burning and destroying villages, towns and cities.

Even though the Germans were coming, Olga and Malamati still had to plant and harvest the fields. If they did not produce and store for the coming months they would starve during the harsh winters. They worked side-by-side in the fields, both dressed in their black clothes like two crows pecking at the land. Heraklis was helping his *Mama* in the fields. He was now nine years old and he was a very hard-working young man.

It was summer time in 1943, and although he was only five years old, Olga had taught Eleftherios to pick the fruit, cut it in halves and lay it on old sheets on the ground to dry, while he kept the flies and birds away, in the back yard of the half- built house that they had.

Olga had heard that the Germans were marching down from the mountains that day and the villagers hurried to go and hide. Malamati had left her as she hurried to hide before the Germans marched through the village. Olga knew that she, too, had to take her son and go. She piled all her picked vegetables into the baskets and put Heraklis on the mule and headed for home to make sure that Eleftherios was safe.

Malamati got home earlier so she told Eleftherios "Come with me we must hide; the Germans are coming". However, Eleftherios told her, "I am not leaving the fruit. *Mama* told me I must look after it".

Malamati was frustrated as she knew they had to hide. She told Eleftherios, "If you will not leave at least get under the basket and you can still keep an eye on the fruit".

As Olga and Heraklis neared their home, they heard Eleftherios screaming out at the top of his voice, "Stop stealing our fruit! That is ours!" Olga hurried the mule towards the back of the house to where her young son was yelling.

As she turned the corner of the house she could see two young German soldiers picking and eating the juicy apricots and laughing. She could not see her son, but she could hear him. The young voice continued, "*Mama*, come quick, come quick. They are stealing our fruit".

Suddenly one of the German soldiers pointed his gun to shoot at the basket from where the voice was coming. Both soldiers were laughing and joking, but they certainly meant business and were ready to shoot Eleftherios.

Olga felt that God had given her the strength as she raced towards her son's voice yelling out, "Please, please do not shoot, he is only a child. Do not shoot him".

The two soldiers ran towards the basket at the same time as Olga did. She reached the basket first, lifted it and grabbed Eleftherios into her arms. The young soldiers spoke in German, laughing and pointing the gun at them. They were aiming to shoot both Olga and her sons.

"*Verrater! Verrater!* (Traitor! Traitor!)", the soldiers were calling out. Holding a handful of ripe apricots in their hands, they ate and laughed and spat the pips out towards Olga.

Olga stared at them, not moving. She could not understand them, but she felt like an old crow because she was dressed in black and she was ready to attack if they dared to hurt her boys. She prayed continuously and silently, saying over and over, "*Oh, Christos nika ta panda,*" (Christ conquers all) holding her son closer. The Germans pointed their guns at them as they laughed and teased them with the guns in their hands.

Suddenly a stern voice called out, "Rolf! Gerhard!" The German captain was calling out to them from the road. The soldiers walked away, arrogantly spitting the apricot seeds at Olga as they went. She just stood there, motionless, until she could not hear them any more. She walked slowly into her half-built house and collapsed onto the dirt floor of the cellar, thanking God for their survival.

Olga decided there and then that she belonged in her own house. The boys were growing and needed their own home, as Malamati's house had become so crowded. Olga knew that as she had no husband she had to make the decisions. So she moved into her half-built home in that part of the cellar where the animals were. She made some rough beds for her children with pieces of old timber. She had an old combustion stove for cooking and heating and put grass mats on the dirt floor. It was not much, but it was her home, and the friction created by living with her mother-in-law was gone. Her harvest was stored in the other part of the cellar.

Olga was really worried about her parents and with the Germans in the area she was concerned about travelling to Florina to take them their weekly provisions.

Olga found out later that her *Baba*, Zacharia, who had been working in the bakery with his wife, was not well. He was visited daily by the Germans and, if the bread had been baked, they would simply help themselves to all the bread.

Zacharia was annoyed when one of the Germans also took his cigarettes. He had a little box where he kept his homemade cigarettes, made from the tobacco Olga had often provided him.

One day the Germans came and took all the bread again, but this time one of the soldiers lingered on. He was the one who always demanded cigarettes from Zacharia.

Zacharia would milk snakes and catch leeches to use in various remedies he made, so he was not afraid of creepy, crawly things.

"Zacharia, can I have one of your homemade cigarettes?" the German soldier said.

"Sure," Zacharia replied. This time he handed his cigarette box to the soldier and stood back.

The young man opened the box and tried to lift a cigarette when suddenly all the cigarettes came alive as the box was full of little snakes and they started moving. The young German soldier ran out screaming. And Zacharia had a wonderful chuckle and never saw the soldier again.

In Florina the Germans rounded up all the Jews, the gypsies, intellectuals, resistance members and branded the Jews with the Star of David and put them on the trains and sent them off to Auschwitz in Poland.

Zacharia took many chances and went out of his way to help people. One of them was his nephew who was an intellectual and an only son. He had married a Jewish girl, but his parents did not want to know him as he had changed his faith from a Christian to Jewish. When the Germans were rounding up the Jewish people Zacharia rescued his nephew and young wife. He hid them and helped them to escape. Later he heard that they had immigrated to New Zealand.

The Germans had orders to round up all the men and young boys in the village of Tropaioukhos and had taken them into the church to shoot them. This happened to many villages throughout Greece as they felt these men and boys were a threat to them. Olga and many other women in the village prayed for a miracle and sure enough all the men and young boys were released. All the villagers were very thankful as they felt that this German captain was not as harsh, as they had heard that in many other villages the men and boys had been shot.

If the houses were big enough German soldiers were billeted in with the people. The families usually all slept in one room while the soldiers took over the other rooms. The people were thankful that all of the men were gentlemen like their captain.

#14
Olga's Mother's prediction

Olga tried to visit her parents as often as she could, at least once a month. She felt that it was important for the boys to see their grandparents, aunts and cousins. Her elder sister Giannoulla had six boys and one girl; it was always a joy to catch up with all her sisters and their families. Her other sisters, Sapfo and Anna, always spoilt her boys and they enjoyed having Olga visit.

Unfortunately their *Mama*, Olympia, had been very sick lately and Olga was very concerned for her. On one particular visit, Olga held her *Mama's* hand and just sat beside her. Her *Mama* opened her eyes and said, "Olga, your husband Gianni is alive; he will come back. I *know* that he will come back soon. You will also have a daughter; I want you to give her my name as it has been in our family for generations. Your great-grandmother came from Olympia to Thrace and married your great-grandfather, and when she had a girl she named her Olympia. Every eldest son has carried this name, but unfortunately all your brothers were killed in the war. I want you to carry the family name. Olga, promise me that you will do this".

"*Mama*, please rest." Olga thought that her *Mama* was losing the plot. How can her husband be alive? Didn't she receive the telegram from the Army advising her that Gianni was lost? He was presumed dead. The grief and agony Olga had gone through had turned her hair white overnight. Living with her mother-in-law did not help matters. Life was very hard for Olga. There were arguments and fights over her children because they were annoying their grandmother, Malamati.

The land that Olga and Gianni had worked so hard belonged to her sons. It was their heritage from their *Baba*. She would not leave and, if she could, where would she go? Hadn't she been wearing black clothes for mourning for the past few years? How could she tell her *Mama* that there would not be a daughter, a daughter that she also wanted? She and her sons had to make the best of each day in order to survive. Gianni had gone and he would not be back. She was a widow and it was only with God's help that she made it through each day. Olga wanted to tell her *Mama* this, but was afraid it would worry her. She tried to calm her by holding her hand and gently telling her to rest and not to worry. She knew that her *Mama* did not have long to live. "*Mama*, do not worry, just rest."

"Olga, Olga! You are not listening to me. I know that Gianni is alive and he will be back and you will have the daughter you want. You must name her Olympia. If you do not name her, my curse is on you. Olga! Promise me you will name your daughter Olympia."

Olga's *Mama*, Olympia, was very sure that Gianni would return and that her granddaughter would take her name.

Olga held her *Mama's* hand and just sat with her, reassuring her to calm her. Olga asked herself *what harm could she do?* So she promised the old lady. "Yes, *Mama*, I promise that I will name my daughter after you, do not worry". Olga thought *does it matter if her Mama's wish was never to be granted, after all, her husband was lost.* She just said it to keep her Mama happy. She was old, what does it matter? She did not believe that her wish could or would ever be accomplished.

"Olga, listen to me! I know with all my heart and soul that the good Lord Jesus has spared Gianni. Always remember this, my daughter, that with these words, *Oh Christos nika ta Panda,* Jesus will always be there to help you. Just ask and he will give you the strength and the courage to overcome all your trials and tribulations. Jesus was there for me when I lost all my six boys. To see the Turkish soldier kill my elder twins and my parents when they came through Margarra was a nightmare. But then when we were trying to get on the boats they grabbed the other two boys and threw them into the water. It was the most horrible anguish any mother could witness. Then one by one I lost the others as we were pushed from here to there with no food or shelter, into refugee camps. As the war raged we lost everything, lands, homes and children. It was only with God's help that we survived. Always remember those words; they will give you the strength and courage to keep going."

#15

Eleftherios Wants a Father

In October 1944 the German forces were withdrawing from Greece and the Greek Government had returned from exile. Men were returning home from the war and life in the village, and all over Greece, was slowly returning to normal.

It was a Sunday and Olga had just finished cleaning her little home when Eleftherios came running in, calling out, "*Mama! Mama!*"

Olga came running out of the house terrified that something had happened to her younger son. "What is wrong with you?" she called out.

"There are so many *Babas* gathering at the church," Eleftherios replied excitedly.

"Yes. I know. It is the 28th of October and we are celebrating *'Ochi'* Day, which is the day the Metaxas Government had refused the Italians and the Germans to come through Greece. There is a memorial service today at the church." Olga bent down and picked up her son. She held him and looked into his shiny brown eyes as she listened to her son's pleading.

"*Mama*, everyone has a *Baba*. Can we have one of those *Babas* for us, please, *Mama*? I'd like to have a *Baba*, please! Please, *Mama*! There are lots of *Babas* at the church. Everyone is calling them *Pater* (Father)."

Olga's heart was aching. How could she help her son after he had lost his *Baba* when so very young? He had not seen his *Baba* since he was a toddler. She tried to tell him, "My son, my dear son, those *Babas* (*Paters*) are priests. Eleftherios, they are all gathered for the memorial service at the church for the many soldiers and innocent people who died during the war. Your *Baba* was one of them; he was lost in the war my son." Olga tried to explain that to her six-year-old. How can she tell him that he will never know his *Baba* as he was only a baby when his *Baba* went off to war?

"Please! Please, *Mama;* let's get a *Baba*. I want one! Please!" Eleftherios pleaded.

Olga held her son tightly in her arms as she prayed silently *'Oh Lord Jesus, please help us'*.

#16
Gianni's return

Olga had left the two boys working in the fields with their grandmother Malamati, while she went to be with her mother who was still very sick.

It was early in May 1945 and Olga was sitting by her *Mama's* bedside. Her *Mama* kept repeating over and over "Gianni is alive. He is coming back and you will have the daughter you have always wanted. You will name her Olympia or the family curse will be on you". Olga's *Mama* mumbled this continuously.

"Olga, don't listen to her, she has been delirious for the past few months repeating that over and over. We have not been able to get through to her that Gianni has been killed in the war," Zacharia said to his daughter.

Suddenly there was a knock on the door. Olga went to the door and opened it. She could not believe it. Gianni was standing in the doorway. Olga's mouth dropped, "My God, you are alive!"

"Is that how you greet your husband?" exclaimed Gianni.

Olga hugged him and her tears were flowing down her cheeks.

"Olga, where are you? Come quickly!" her father called from the bedroom.

Holding Gianni's hand and with her tears still flowing, Olga led him into her *Mama's* bedroom.

Olympia lifted her head slightly and said, "Gianni, my son, you are home at last. I knew you would return". Gianni dropped to his knees and holding his mother-in-law's hand said, "*Mama*, I am home. We need to celebrate. You have to get better now."

"My son I am at peace at last, I am going home… Gianni, you will have a daughter and you will name her Olympia, the family name," Olympia whispered as she closed her eyes and died in Gianni's arms.

The whole family was in a state of shock. It was both a sad and a happy occasion for all of them as they cried and laughed together. Zacharia knew he had to organise the funeral and he asked his son-in-law, "Gianni, my son, will you please come with me to the church to see the priest so that we can arrange for the funeral?"

"Yes, *Baba*," Gianni replied. Even though he was tired and wanted to rest he knew that he must help.

"Olga and Sapfo please clean and wash your *Mama's* body for the viewing," Zacharia asked.

"All right, *Baba,*" they mumbled in unison, as they both felt numb.

How in the world were they going to do that they both thought and looked at each other.

"Anna, I want you to do a very important job. Please go and tell your older sister Giannoulla that your *Mama* has passed away and to notify all the relatives and friends for us. Would you be a brave girl and do that?" Zacharia asked his younger daughter.

"Yes, *Baba*," Anna replied with tears running down her face.

When everyone left, Olga and Sapfo looked at each other and Sapfo said, "Oh Olga, what are we going to do?"

"We will wash and clean our *Mama's* body and dress her. We will do it!" Olga said firmly.

It was the hardest thing for both of them. Although they were both crying, they were supporting each other and so were able to get through this most difficult task of their lives. They then laid Olympia, their *Mama*, on the lounge divan for the family and friends to visit and pay their last respects. They both cried and cried while doing this.

There was a knock on the door. Sapfo opened it and saw three ladies dressed in black. Sapfo said sobbing "How can I help you, ladies?"

"We are professional mourners. Our fees are not much. We can shed a lot of tears for your loved one at the funeral," they said in unison. Sapfo's mouth dropped and she glared at them. She could not believe what she had heard. She was about to yell at them, when Olga called out firmly from behind Sapfo, "Thank you, ladies, but we don't need you," and shut the door quickly.

"The cheek of them! I would have punched them if you did not interrupt! As if we cannot cry ourselves! And how in the world did they find out that our *Mama* had died? Oh Olga, can you tell me? Oh, the cheek of them!" Sapfo yelled. She was very angry.

"I don't know about you, Sapfo, but I have heard that there are professional mourners. You and I have shed enough tears while preparing our *Mama's* body to flood the river. Even though I know she is at peace at last and she is with our dear Lord, our *Mama* had suffered for a long time, but she was hanging in there until Gianni came home. That's incredible, I can't believe it," Olga said.

"I do wish that *Baba* and Gianni would hurry back from the church, Olga, as you and I have to look after the people coming to view our *Mama's* body. I don't know if I can handle them," Sapfo muttered.

"Of course we can Sapfo. She looks at peace at last. *Mama* was in a lot of pain for a long time," Olga reassured Sapfo. "I remember each time I visited her and tried to help she would tell me that I had enough to do in looking after my boys and a home without coming to help her. She was so independent; she would not let anyone do things for her. Even though she was in pain, she dragged herself around doing her work."

Family and friends came and paid their respects. They all sat around talking and crying and sharing their grief and loss together.

#17
Olympia's funeral

The funeral for Olympia was held on the following day. It was a simple ceremony at the church. It was attended by family and friends who all paid their respects. At the grave-side there was the priest, Zacharia and his daughters and the older grandchildren (Giannoula's sons and one daughter). It was only very close family and friends who were there. They were all very sad and many were crying.

Suddenly Zacharia farted very loudly and then ducked and yelled out, "Look out, a bomb has gone off". He had all his loved ones in hysterics. Olga often said that he had a really wicked sense of humour. With all the trials and tribulations he always tried to make his daughters laugh. Even though tears were needed and it was fine to cry and let out grief and pain, he knew there was always a time to laugh and a time to cry.

After the funeral Olga and Gianni headed back to the village. Both were anxious to see their boys. For Gianni it had been five long years since he had seen them. Olga was hoping that the boys had been a help to Malamati rather than a hindrance. Olga and Gianni walked side-by-side, both deep in thought.

Olga was yearning to know what had happened to Gianni and asked, "Your entire platoon was reported killed, so what happened?"

"We had fought hard and pushed the Italians back to the Albanian border. Then it was very quiet for a couple of days, so the captain picked out another soldier and me to scout the Albanian border. We were dressed in peasants' clothes."

"How terrifying it must have been, to venture into the enemy territory," Olga uttered.

"It was, particularly when the Italians regrouped and attacked our platoon. We heard the fighting as we headed back. But I tripped and fell and broke my nose and my knees."

"My mate tried to cross over the river to reach the platoon, but was caught in the fighting in the middle of the freezing waters. He was taken as a prisoner of war, but died later with pleurisy. I was apparently taken to the prison hospital, but I could not remember as I had suffered concussion from my fall. I did not know who I was and had no identification.

"When they realised that I was a Greek soldier, the Italians put me into the prison camp where the conditions were really bad. There was very little food, no clothes and no toilets. In one little room we ate, slept and relieved ourselves. There were people dying all around me either from starvation or sickness, but thank God I survived. I occupied my hands and my mind by making worry beads. I kept on repeating my Baba's blessing *H Duname Tou Theou na ine panda mazi sou*. I pictured and prayed that I would see my wife and sons again as I repeated the blessing.

"We had no knowledge of how many days or months we spent in prison. The days were all the same and we lost track of time. Then word got around that the Germans were coming through. The conditions were bad enough, but when we heard that, we felt that all hope was lost. I kept on repeating over and over that God's strength was with me. The others kept yelling at me to forget my God as He had forsaken me, but I put my trust in my father's blessing.

"Then one dark night we heard doors opening. A priest came through and helped us escape. He supplied us with warm clothing, as we had to cross the Italian Alps into Switzerland. It was very cold and many lost their lives because of their poor physical condition. The Red Cross took care of the lucky ones who survived. They billeted us to various homes in Switzerland. Food was still scarce, but the Swiss people were kind and helped us recover from our ordeals of prison and the trek over the Alps."

"But why didn't they notify us?" Olga asked.

"As you know, I can't read or write. Often they gave us paperwork to complete, but as I couldn't read, I would put it away," replied Gianni.

#18

GIANNI RETURNS TO THE VILLAGE

Back in the village word had gone ahead that Gianni was alive and was heading home. When Olga and Gianni arrived, there in their yard was a crowd of villagers and lots of children, family and friends to greet Gianni.

"Gianni, my son, you were lost. I had read the telegram. Thank God you are alive. It's incredible, it's a miracle," Malamati exclaimed as she hugged and kissed her son with tears flowing down her cheeks.

The young children all lined up to greet Gianni. Olga said, "Gianni, your sons are anxious to greet you," and she pointed to their two boys, but there were many other boys and girls keen to greet him. Gianni approached anxiously, as he could not recognise his boys because he hadn't seen them for years. The first young boy came towards him and he thought that he must be Heraklis. Gianni went over and hugged him, lifted him into his arms and kissed him. He then approached a younger boy thinking it was Eleftherios, and did the same. Unfortunately it was one of the Deliyannis boys who were cousins. He ended up kissing and hugging all the children as they came to greet him.

Both the boys were fair-haired, but all the cousins looked alike so Gianni assumed the first two boys he had kissed and hugged were both his sons. Well, Eleftherios burst into tears and went to his *Mama* crying. He was deeply hurt. The fact that his *Baba* hadn't recognised him stayed with him all his life. Even though his *Mama* had tried to explain to him that he was only a baby when his *Baba* had gone to the war, and there was no way that his *Baba* would be able to recognise him, especially with all the children crowding around Gianni, Eleftherios could not understand. How could his *Baba* not hug him if it was his *Baba*?

Gianni followed his mother to the old house holding his two sons' hands. Malamati put a spread on for all of them and they exchanged all the news. He also met his brother's wife, Ourania, and their little baby girl, Anna.

Gianni had presents for all of them. He gave his wife, Olga, a Swiss watch, each of the boys a watch and his mother a black jacket. His brother Christopher received the worry beads he had made while in prison. He had also brought a Saint Bernard puppy with him. He was very proud of that puppy and named him Sarko.

The celebrations for Gianni's return finally came to an end. It had been a very taxing day and Gianni said, "I'm tired and the boys look tired. I think we should all go to bed."

Olga and Malamati exchanged glances, and then Olga said, "Gianni, the boys and I have moved into our own house. Come, let's go home."

Gianni looked at Olga and then at his mother wondering what was going on and said "But it's not finished, our home is not finished," protested Gianni. He wanted answers, but he was tired and he did not feel up to finding out right away.

The next day, Olga tried to explain to Gianni that it was very crowded in Malamati's place, and although their home was not finished, at least it was theirs. It was *their* home and the boys could do whatever they wanted instead of causing friction at Malamati's house. This arrangement was so much better.

While Gianni understood, he was disappointed that Olga had to move into their home before it had been completed. He was determined to finish their house. It was not easy, but Gianni and Olga and the boys all worked to make their home more livable.

The boys loved helping their father build the home. Gianni and his sons made the mud bricks with straw and red clay setting them in the moulds, then letting the bricks dry in the sun. Gradually they built the walls and put a roof over their heads.

Eventually Gianni was going to divide the interior into two bedrooms, a living room and a kitchen. At that time it was just one huge room, which was their bedroom, living room and kitchen. All the family lived upstairs and having this extra space was a luxury for them because now they had the downstairs for both the animals and a cellar for their produce. They were in their own home, and although they had very few furnishings, they at least had a roof over their heads. Heating was by the old combustion stove, which was also used for their cooking. This was in the middle of the room.

Building the house had been a very slow process, as they still had to work in the fields. Gianni decided to a build a toilet outside and the neighbours wondered what he was doing. He built the frame, a square box of about four to five feet wide and approximately seven feet high, in the back yard. He then thatched the walls and the roof and put on a door. Inside he had dug a hole and put slate stones from the river on either side of the hole for people to stand on while they squatted to go to the toilet. He then had the excess water from the communal spring flow through to clean the toilet. Then along a little channel that was dug it flowed down to the creek, which was always running at the end of the back yard. A kerosene lamp provided light for the toilet.

Olga was so proud of her backyard toilet as there certainly were no toilets in the other houses; her neighbours all used a potty and then dug a hole in the ground and buried it. This was all very primitive and especially hard during winter when it was minus 10 to 20 degrees and the ground was frozen, but still it was better than going behind the bushes. However, in the middle of winter the water from the spring froze and it was necessary to start using a potty again!

After working in the fields, Olga would stay up until all hours sewing or mending their clothes or knitting jumpers, socks, gloves and caps for the winter. She would spin the wool from the few sheep they had to make their jumpers or would weave rugs or carpets from various rags or spare wool. In the summers she would whitewash the walls and try to be artistic by soaking a rag in colored paint and make various patterns on the walls. Olga made do with very little, but she felt God was always there to provide for their main necessities.

#19
Civil War in Greece

In 1945 a civil war began raging throughout Greece between the royalists and the communists. It caused brothers to fight brothers and fathers to fight sons. During World War II, the communist guerrillas had proven to be strong resistance fighters against the Italians and the Germans. In 1945 their idea was to bring equality to all Greeks. They wanted to eliminate the ruling classes, but now they had begun to fight each other. It was a very dirty war.

Olga and Gianni were starting to see an improvement in their life until Gianni was conscripted back into the army because of the civil war. Gianni had had enough of wars and didn't want anything to do with that war. He had seen enough fighting to last him his lifetime, but by late 1946 he was back in the national army.

Once again, Olga and her two sons were struggling to survive. Olga also found out she was pregnant. Life was not going to be easy again; the war was being fought in nearby towns and villages. Olga still had to work in the fields to plant and harvest her crops. It was the only way her family could survive.

She would harness the bullock early in the morning and then head out to the fields. She would then harness it to the plough in order to plough the fields, while the boys would follow behind to clear the fields of stones and rubbish.

Once that field was ploughed she then would plant the tobacco seedlings, wheat, corn and her various vegetables, such as beans, lentils, garlic, leek, tomatoes, potatoes, onions, cucumbers and various herbs. It was all done by hand and it was very backbreaking work. Olga also had to make sure the irrigation channels were dug deep enough so that she could water her plants. She also worked until late in the evenings, weaving, sewing or knitting. When Gianni was home on leave he was able to share the work, but when he was away again, this was all left up to Olga and the boys.

Olga did not want the boys to miss out on their schooling so she tried to send them off to school as often as she could while she would work by herself in the fields. Olga was so determined that the boys should not miss any schooling she sold whatever possessions she had in order to put them through school. She reached the stage where her last item of value was her wedding ring; she even sold that to put her boys through school. The boys, even though they were young, still helped their *Mama* in the fields before and after school and on weekends. Although Olga was pregnant she never stopped to rest, but worked from dawn through to dusk.

Late one afternoon Eleftherios' teacher approached her and said to her "I know you work very hard, Olga, and want your boys to have an education, but I haven't seen Eleftherios for weeks. I wondered if he was helping you because you have paid his school fees and that is a waste of your money."

Olga was shocked and said, "But how can that be, I send him to school every morning." She was very surprised.

"I thought that would be the case, Olga, but he doesn't turn up in class I assure you. I just don't want you to waste your money. Keep an eye on what he does tomorrow morning," the teacher said.

The next morning Olga and the boys were out very early in the fields. After working for some time she sent the boys off to school. She then followed her younger son and watched him head for school. However, each day a shepherd brought his flock of sheep past the school and took them up in the mountains. Suddenly she saw Eleftherios bend down and hide among the sheep. He, too, headed towards the mountains with the shepherd and his sheep.

In the evening Olga asked Heraklis and Eleftherios, "How was school?"

"It was great *Mama*," they both replied.

"And you learnt lots and are coping with the schoolwork, Eleftherios," she asked him, looking straight at him.

He looked at her and said slowly, "Yes, *Mama*".

Olga stared at her son. His round face looked at her very innocently so she said to him, "And did you enjoy your day on the mountains with the sheep, Eleftherios?"

He put his head down and said, "*Mama*, I don't like school. I would rather help you".

"Eleftherios! Eleftherios! Your *Baba* and I would like you to learn to read and write. Life is not easy if you cannot do that," Olga said to him.

"But I can read and write. That is enough for me. I do not want to go to school any more. I do not like it," Eleftherios said.

"What do you want to do, Eleftherios?" Olga asked, very frustrated.

"*Mama*, I want to help you," he said proudly.

"You both help me already and I am managing at the moment. Your *Baba* and I would like you to finish school or at least learn a trade. What would you like to be, Eleftherios, if you do not want to go to school?"

"I want to be a shoemaker, *Mama*," Eleftherios said.

"Eleftherios, I want you to promise me that you will finish grade 6. I will then find you a job as an apprentice to a shoemaker. I will keep my promise to you, but I want your word that you will not miss school again. I promised your *Baba* to do my best to keep you at school. You know that I am working hard to put you both through school. Please do not disappoint me. It would be much easier for me to have you helping me in the fields," Olga said.

"I promise you I will finish grade 6 and then I can become a shoemaker," Eleftherios said.

#20

Olga has a daughter

In June 1947 Olga was heavy with her third child. She was on top of the hay wagon trying to fill the barn with hay. All day she had had labor pains. When the pains came, she stopped working for a few minutes, then took a deep breath and continued with her work. The pains increased as she was on top of the wagon.

Suddenly her water broke and *Thea* Mersina, who lived next-door, saw the blood and water flowing down her legs. "My child, you are having the baby! For goodness sake, get to bed! I'll call the midwife," she yelled from the fence.

"I can't. I have to get the hay into the barn," Olga replied.

"We will do it for you. Now get to bed! *Marree! Maree! Kori di kanis'* ('For heaven's sake, daughter, what are you doing?') It was a favorite saying of *Thea* Mersina's – which she exclaimed, helping Olga into the house as the tiny baby slid into the world. *Thea* and Malamati helped her into bed. They cleaned the baby and tied the umbilical cord.

This is how I was born – almost on the top of a haystack!

"It's a girl! Your wish has come true!" Malamati exclaimed.

When Heraklis arrived home from school he was annoyed and yelled at his *Mama*. He was now 13 years old. "We haven't enough food to eat! We barely survive! And you have brought another mouth to feed into this world."

Olga knew that her son made sense, but she wanted a little girl so much. She didn't mind working harder to feed them.

Gianni managed to get a couple of days leave to come and see his wife. He too was thrilled to have a baby daughter. He said to Olga, "Your *Mama's* prediction has come true and God has granted you your wish, Olga. You have the daughter you have wanted for so long."

While Gianni was on leave they decided to baptise their daughter. They went to see the godparents again and explained their *Mama's* wish. They had to name me 'Olympia' and he agreed.

But once again at the church the priest asked what the baby's name was to be and the godfather called out, "Anastasia".

Olga was really angry and yelled out, "My *Mama's* curse is on your family if you do not call my daughter Olympia".

The godfather relented and said to the priest, "We better call the baby Olympia".

So Olga and Gianni at last had a child named after Olga's *Mama*.

Giagia Olympia and Papou Zacharia, their oldest daughter Giannoula before the World War I.

Giagia Olympian and Papou Zacharia and Thea Giannoula
in the refuge camp in Thesaloniki, 1922.

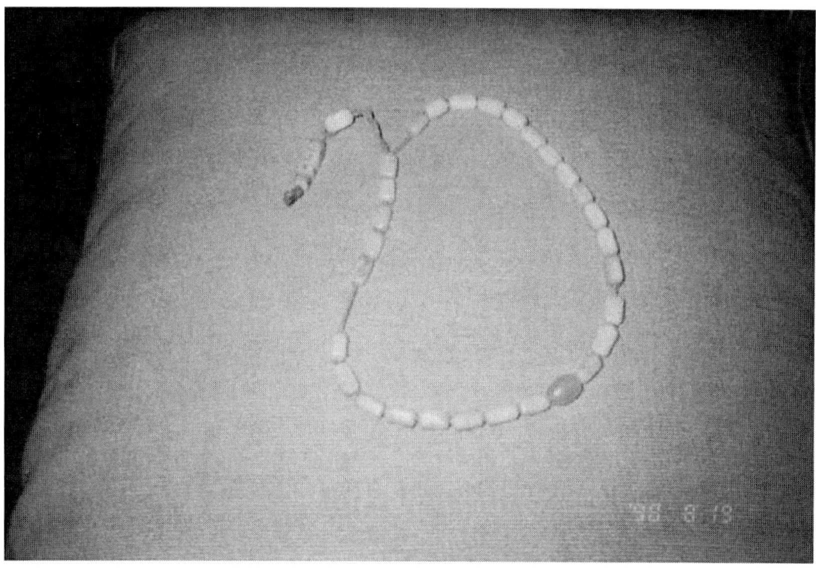

Baba's Kombologi (worry Beads). Which he made in the Italian Prisoner of War Camp.

Mama, Baba and Heraklis, 1937.

Mama, Giagia, Eleftherios and Heraklis in Florina, 1944.

Family before we migrated to Australia

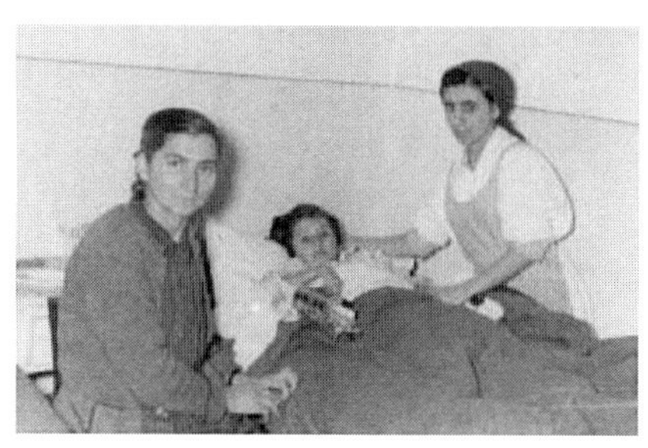

I am in Thesaloniki Hospital

In front of our house in Tropaioukhos with Giagia Malamati

Our Strawberry Farm at Tropaioukhos

Eleftherios, Mamma and me
during the Civil War

First Easter at Tropaioukhos.
The 4 of us.

Eleftherios and Heraklis, Heraklis migrating to Australia 1954.

Skaugum, the boat we arrived in Melbourne 1955.

All the family in front of the Greek Church. Our first Easter together, 1956..

Mama and Baba when he retired in Melbourne

Anastasia, Anna and me, in front of my Baba's house in Kouvouklia in 2008.
The house still locked since they left it in 1922. Photo: Heather Forman

#21
The Bomb Shelter

The civil war raged on. Many families had sons and daughters fighting each other, with innocent people dying. But people still planted and harvested to feed their families. Whenever the fighting was close, all the villagers ran to their rough bomb shelters, which were usually very crowded. *Mama* always sent my brothers and me (I was only three months old!) with them to the shelter for protection, while she continued working in the fields.

On one occasion it was so crowded that Heraklis put the quilt down outside the entrance to the shelter then placed Eleftherios and me on it and lay beside us. We were all cuddled together. There was fighting raging fiercely nearby and it was impossible to sleep. Heraklis held us and huddled as close as possible to the bomb-shelter door.

Suddenly Alexis yelled out, “My God, that’s Olga’s children out there!” and pulled the quilt with the children on it inside the bomb shelter, just in time as a bomb exploded near the entrance. A couple of the teenage girls had made a swing with a blanket and tried to keep me quiet as I was crying all the time and other people said to the boys,

"Next time do not bring the baby with you, do you hear? Leave her with your *Mama*".

When *Mama* heard what had happened she was devastated. She then sent Heraklis, Eleftherios and me to live with her *Baba* in Florina, since my *Baba* was still in the army.

It was a big responsibility for *Papou*, but he loved us and was pleased to help. *Thea* Anna, his youngest daughter, went to college to be a teacher while Heraklis started high school. Eleftherios was to start a trade when he finished primary school, as was agreed with *Mama*.

The war had become very fierce with brothers fighting brothers, fathers fighting sons, relations fighting each other. The *Andartes* (the communist guerrillas) were gathering all the children and sending them over the border.

Papou hid Heraklis, Eleftherios, *Thea* Anna (his younger daughter) and me in the ceiling of his house when the *Pedomasoma* (the gathering of the children) came through. The communist guerrillas were taking all the children and sending them to the communist bloc countries, placing them all in various orphanages, while the older ones were sent for indoctrination. *Papou* fed me by dipping the corner of a handkerchief in lentil soup and letting me suck on that to keep me quiet until the guerrillas had passed by.

By the end of 1948, the guerrillas had gathered more than 28,000 children from their parents and had sent them to camps throughout the communist bloc.

After leaving Florina, the *Andartes* came through Tropaioukhos, rampaging through the houses and destroying the few possessions the villagers had. At *Mama's* house they barged through the front door demanding to know where the children were.

"They are not here!" cried *Mama*.

The *Andartes* pushed passed her and went through the house with their machetes and bayonets slashing furniture and containers. *Mama* could not stand it any more and yelled at them "Do you think that I am hiding children or mice here?"

"Shut up, woman, and bring your three children out," one of them called out to her, as he continued to smash everything. Olga was terrified, but intrigued as to how they even knew how many children she had.

"Do you have to destroy the place? I told you that the children are not here!" she screamed at them.

They laughed and pushed her against the wall as they said, "Not to worry, we have your children rounded up already, as we have gathered all the children from all over the country and from every school. We have gone through Florina already and gathered them from there".

Again, even though *Mama* had never seen these men before, they knew she had connections in Florina. How was that so?

"We are sending them to be educated, because we need new recruits," the guerillas informed her.

Mama could not sleep that night, worrying whether or not her children had been taken from her *Baba's* house or the school. There was no telephone to call her *Baba* so early in the morning she headed for Florina. It was still dark; she ran and walked as fast as she could all the way. As she reached the edge of Florina a big, black dog, foaming at the mouth suddenly appeared and attacked her. *Mama* screamed as she fought off the sick dog. Its teeth got a vice grip on her hip so she grabbed it by the ears to try to make the dog release its teeth from her hip. People came running out of their homes and one young man shot the dog. *Mama* was on the road bleeding badly, unable to move. Some of the people lifted her and raced her to the hospital, which was already overcrowded with wounded soldiers.

She had lost a lot of blood and was in danger of losing her leg or her life. The doctors called *Papou,* who sat by *Mama's* bed encouraging her not to give up.

Despite *Mama's* fever her screams were "My children! My children! Are they safe?" she screamed out again and again.

"Olga, your children are all safe. I hid them in the ceiling and the *Andartes* did not find them. Please, Olga, you have to get better. Your children need you," *Papou* tried to reassure and calm his daughter.

Papou was on his knees beside his daughter and he prayed loudly, "Lord Jesus, please, please take me. I am an old man. Let my daughter live as her children need her. Please Lord".

Baba immediately came home on leave. His commanders told him they did not believe that his wife would pull through the night, as the dog had been sick.

Now both *Baba* and *Papou* were on their knees beside *Mama's* bed, both of them praying for her recovery by repeating over and over again "*Oh Christos nika ta panda*" (Christ conquers all)

Mama was unconscious for days and it was touch and go if she would pull through. Slowly she regained consciousness and the doctors were surprised that she did. But she was very weak. She stayed with her *Baba* to recover while my *Baba* returned to the army.

Papou looked after all of us, his daughter Anna, *Mama*, Heraklis, Eleftherios and me. What a handful! But at least *Mama* was slowly recovering.

As soon as *Mama* was able to get around she went back to the village, but we stayed behind as she was only just able to look after herself.

#22

Life in Florina with Papou Zacharia

Mama returned to her home and although her health was not the best she struggled and tried to cope with the workload. She visited us and her father in Florina as often as she could. However, the house and fields were neglected and were in a bad state. *Baba* was still in the army and was unable to help his family. Most families were suffering as the men were either in the army or had been wounded and lost legs or arms (or killed), as there were many mines that had been planted by the enemy. Many families were struggling to survive.

Papou continued to look after me and Heraklis. He went to high school in Florina, while Eleftherios was sent to a boarding school at Baxestsifliki, outside the seaside city of Thessaloniki. Some boys whose fathers served in the army were sent to the boarding school to help out the families.

Papou had built a strong bond with us, especially with me. I was spoilt by all of them, especially by Heraklis and *Thea* Anna. *Thea* had married a young policeman, George, and he too kept an eye on me.

As I grew up *Papou* would hold my little hand and take me up on to the mountain collecting various herbs and plants, which he used to make his many ointments. He showed me how to catch snakes and milk them and then would walk along the creek with me as he caught leeches, which he used to put on to patients to draw out any bad or infected blood. Growing up with *Papou* taught me to love and respect animals and nature. It was the best time of my life and that passion stayed with me all my life. I often saw him set people's broken arms using little pieces of sticks. After he put the arm back in place he would make a plaster by mixing up the various ointments, which he then put around the arm. The little sticks held the arm in place and then he would bandage it.

I followed *Papou* everywhere, as I was fascinated by his patience and his caring for people and animals. When he was in the garden he showed me how to plant seeds and look after plants. Together we would carry rocks from the creek and put a border around his little patches of various types of herbs.

The best part was at the end of the day when he would hold my hand and we would walk up the mountain, sit down on a large rock and *Papou* would say to me, "Time to listen to the birds and animals. Be still so that we do not frighten any wild animals". I would be thrilled if I saw a hare or when a porcupine would come out slowly from its hiding place with its spikes sticking up and its little legs waddling as fast as it could go, heading to find food. *Papou* would put his finger on his lips "Shhh, just listen, little one, and enjoy God's miracle".

We would watch the beautiful sunset and then he would talk to God from there. He would then hold my hand and slowly we would walk back home. I never remembered going to church with *Papou*. He would tell me that God was with us all the time and we could talk to God about everything, and especially in this sacred place where we sat every evening on this huge rock, our meditating rock.

I was a very mischievous child, especially when it came to water. I loved playing with water and not too far from *Papou's* house was a communal spring water tap that had a long water trough for the animals to drink. Well, to me it was my swimming pool. Whenever I could, I would play in that water trough. Heraklis had made me a little boat out of paper and I was dying to sail my boat on the water. While all the family was having an afternoon nap, I sneaked out of the house. It was my opportunity to go and try my boat, even though they had told me that I had to go with one of them to the water trough. I was impatient and wanted to see how my boat sailed; I just had to go and try it. I was having such a wonderful time floating my little boat on the water, but the boat was floating away from me. As I reached out to grab it, I fell in with my head in the water and my legs dangling out over the edge of the trough.

Someone grabbed me and pulled me out and yelled at me, "Olympia! Haven't we told you over and over again not to go to the water by yourself?" It was *Theo* George yelling at me and he held me upside down trying to get the water out of me. I coughed and spluttered and was not impressed with him. He was spanking my bottom as well. He then put me down and said, "Olympia, where did spanking come from?"

"From Paradise, *Theo* George," I muttered. (The Greeks have a saying, '*To Xhlo Bgeke apo to Paradiso.* Spanking comes from Paradise) to teach children discipline. I loved to make mud pies near the trough or float things on the water, and both my *Papou* and *Theo* George had rescued me from the water trough on numerous occasions.

I loved having my meals with *Papou*. He had a low, round table to eat from and we all sat around on cushions. He always crossed himself as he started the meals by thanking God for the food before we commenced each meal and he taught me to cross myself. He would tell me, "Olympia, put two fingers with your thumb together; they are the symbol of the Father, Son and Holy Spirit, and then cross yourself to thank God for everything you have and the food that you eat".

We all shared our food. We would dip the crusty bread that *Papou* always broke and passed around. He never believed in cutting it with the knife. We dipped that in the salad (to soak up the olive oil that was used quite liberally in a Greek salad) or in our soups. I loved sharing my food with *Papou* and he always finished the meal with a prayer and crossed himself, thanking God for the food and for being able to share time with each other. Sharing time together was very important for *Papou* as it was a fun time when they shared the events of the day.

Unfortunately this was not to last as *Papou* became very ill and *Mama* came to stay to look after her *Baba*. *Mama* would reprimand me as I still wanted to share my food with *Papou* as I had been doing up until that time. I would take the little bowl of lentil soup to him and give him a spoonful of it and take a spoonful for myself. We would share time together again. But *Mama* would say, “Olympia, leave your *Papou* alone! He is old and he is sick; you cannot eat out of his plate”.

This was devastating for me, not being able to share food with my *Papou* and all the things that I had shared in the past.

Not long after *Papou* was sick I caught a very bad cold and was sick with an extremely high temperature and suffered a convulsion. Having a convulsion was not pleasant, and *Mama* had never seen anyone having one and she started screaming as she held me and cried, not knowing what to do, yelling “Jesus, please do not take my daughter”.

Papou, as sick as he was, got up took me in his arms and put his fingers in my mouth, pulled my tongue out and then he said to *Mama,* “Olga, fetch some water and we will give Olympia a cool bath to bring her temperature down”. They bathed me and then *Papou* put me into bed and he put a face washer on to my forehead that was dipped in vinegar to keep my temperature down. He then kneeled beside my bed and prayed.

Papou had often said to us do whatever you can and then pray and he did just that, even though he was very sick. “Lord Jesus, please take me, not my precious little one. I am old and I have had my days. Please, please Lord, take me and look after Olympia. She is so young; she has a lifetime ahead of her”. He then repeated, over and over ‘*Oh Christos Nika Ta Panda. Oh Christos Nika Ta Panda*’. (Christ conquers all.)

When I had recovered, and was annoying everyone again, *Mama* sent me to her sister Anna in Kastoria. *Thea* Anna was posted to Kastoria as a teacher and her husband was sent there as a policeman, so I stayed with them for a while. *Mama* travelled back and forth from Tropaioukhos to Florina while she shared looking after her *Baba* with her sister, Giannoula, or Giannoula's daughter, Berberka, the eldest granddaughter.

Kastoria is some 200 miles west of Thessaloniki. It is one of the most beautiful towns in Greece surrounded by Lake Orestiada and snow-capped mountains. It was a lovely place with the town overlooking the lake. I loved to walk or run along the lake and had lots and lots of water in which to play. Sometimes I would sit and fish with my *Theo* George and that was a great joy to me, especially when I caught a fish; I would squeal with joy. I enjoyed being with them as *Thea* and *Theo* were very good to me, but I did miss my *Papou.*

Thea Anna and *Theo* George went to Florina and left me with a young student and his family. He was *Thea* Anna's student. I wanted to go with them to see *Papou,* but they would not take me. I was so annoyed that I played up with that family. Each time they tried to dress me I would jump on their lovely spring bed and would not let them dress me. I would yell at them, "I can dress myself. My *Papou* taught me to do that." (Even though I would still put my sandals on the wrong feet.)

When my *Theo* and *Thea* come back, *Thea* sat me on her lap and told me, "*Papou* Zacharia has died". I knew what that meant as often *Papou* and I would bury animals that we found dead. *Papou* always checked to make sure that they were not breathing. He would say to me, "If they are not breathing they are dead". He would then tell me, "They have gone to be with Jesus and one day we will all be with Jesus".

When my cousin Thomas visited us (he was *Thea* Giannoula's son) he always carried rabbits and pigeons in his jacket. I loved it when he visited as I cuddled and held these rabbits or pigeons. He gave me a pet rabbit; *Papou* and I named him Asproulli (White). *Papou* also built a little cage for my Asproulli and that was where I would feed my rabbit and then put him to bed. I loved that rabbit and carried it everywhere, but during one night a fox had tried to get in his little cage, and *Papou* had heard the noise. The fox had killed the rabbit, but was not able to eat it, as *Papou* had chased the fox away. I cried and cried that my rabbit had died. *Papou* and I had to bury it, and so we dug a little hole under a tree and buried little Asproulli and then covered him with dirt and put some flowers on the top to make it look pretty. *Papou* then said the prayers and we put a little cross on the grave. He then sat me on his lap and said to me, "Olympia, it is all right to cry because you miss your friend, but always remember that your rabbit is in God's green garden and one day we will all be there to gather and celebrate. Jesus has a special place for all of us in Heaven".

When *Thea* Anna and *Theo* George told me that *Papou* had died, I started crying and said, "I want my *Papou*; I love *Papou* and I did not want him to die". *Thea* Anna just held me tightly in her arms while I cried and then she cried with me. I looked into her eyes and said to *Thea,* "It's all right to cry because we miss *Papou,* but he is all right. We will all be together one day," and she gave me a big hug. *Thea* Anna and *Theo* George looked at me and then said, "Who told you this?" I replied "*Papou* told me that when my rabbit Asproulli died," and again I hugged each one of them and told them it was all right, they were allowed to cry. They both looked at me puzzled. They had not realised that dear *Papou* had already prepared me for this occasion.

I then told *Thea* and *Theo* of the times when I would sit on the large rock with *Papou* and he would talk to God and he would say, "Let's talk to God". He would say to God, "Lord Jesus, I am looking forward to being with you, Lord Jesus, but only in your timing. Lord, please Lord, I know you are looking after all my boys, my lovely Olympia and I want to be with you Lord one day. I am looking forward to seeing all my boys and my dear Olympia, my love, Asproulli our dear friend and all my other loved ones". And like a parrot I then repeated *Papou's* prayer.

They both looked at me and just cried and hugged me.

#23
Eleftherios in Boarding School

At first my brother Eleftherios enjoyed the boarding school at Baxestsifliki. He often mentioned that at the start the food was good and he also enjoyed the schooling, but as time went on things changed. The quality and the quantity of the food slowly decreased and often all the children would go hungry to bed. Many suffered from this and some of them in their free time would try to catch fish or shellfish to survive. But then they would get into trouble for leaving the school grounds.

Eleftherios had a letter from Heraklis saying that our *Papou* Zacharia had died and he wanted to go to the funeral, but the principal would not allow it. He said that Eleftherios was too young to go to the funeral and he also needed his parent to come and take him as he could not just go by himself. He would also need money to travel and the principal said that they had no funds for that kind of travel. Eleftherios could not understand this because when he came to the boarding school all the boys had travelled from their villages by themselves.

The Government was supposed to be paying for this as all their *Babas* were in the army. It was a boarding school to help these families, but they were told that all the money had been used up or that someone at the school had possibly misused the funds. He was very upset and cried. The teacher told him he was being a sook and he got into trouble for that. He was sent to bed that night, not even having the watery soup that they had been getting for the past few months.

My *Thea* Sapfo had married George Karousos, a soldier who lived in Thessaloniki. They had a baby boy, Spiros, in May 1948. But she continued working as a nurse as she loved her work and was very dedicated in her career. She worked by visiting various schools, helping with vaccinations and checking children's health. She heard that at Baxestsifliki the children were actually dying from malnutrition. She was very concerned and decided to visit Eleftherios.

When she got to the school she asked to see her nephew Eleftherios, but they refused to let her. They told her that only his parents could do that. She showed them her papers and said that she was his *Thea*. But they said they had strict rules not to allow these boys to go to anyone but their parents.

Thea Sapfo was only 4'11", but she had a very determined streak in her. She was used to dealing with wounded soldiers and knew how to handle them. That was how she had met *Theo* George. He had been wounded in the civil war and needed a plate in his head; she had got to know him when she was working at the hospital and ended up marrying him. He came from a wealthy family. His brothers were doctors and his *Baba* was the Mayor of Thessaloniki. She really did not want to go to her in-laws for help, but she could see no other way she could get her nephew out. She felt there was something wrong for them not to let her see her nephew.

She then approached her father-in-law and asked him for help. He made a few calls and then he told her to go and take the boy and that if she had any more trouble to let him know.

When she got to the school this time they welcomed her and just could not do enough for her, offering her a coffee while they got her nephew. It was obvious that the staff only showed respect for her because of her father-in-law. She was disgusted.

She got Eleftherios, but could not believe how thin he was; he looked taller for his age simply because he was all skin and bones. She was not happy with his condition and reported it to the authorities. I believe the authorities looked into it and the rest of the boys were either sent home, if they could be, or the ones who stayed behind were treated better than they were before.

Thea Sapfo kept Eleftherios at her home for a while as she felt he certainly needed to put some meat on him before he went back to Florina. My brother was always thankful for *Thea* turning up when she did as all the boys were starving. He enjoyed the time he had with his *Thea* and *Theo*. My uncle worked as a tram driver and now and then would take Eleftherios with him for a ride. It was a time when he did not have to work or fend for himself and he had many happy memories of staying with *Thea* Sapfo and *Theo* George.

Thea Sapfo had been in touch with *Thea* Anna in Kastoria with whom I was staying and told her that she would be sending my brother back to Florina by train. She asked if *Thea* Anna would pick him up at the Florina station as *Thea* Anna had told her that she would be taking me back to the village. *Thea* Anna and I travelled by bus to Florina and I kept saying, "*Thea,* are we nearly there?" as I was looking forward to seeing my brother. We got off the bus and then walked to the train station. We then had to wait for the train to come from Thessaloniki. When the train came we looked at all the people coming out and waited for Eleftherios. When I saw him I was so excited and ran and hugged him as I was thrilled to see him again. He picked me up and said, "Olympia, haven't you grown? You are a big girl now!" And I nodded and showed him five fingers, as I was five now. It was wonderful to see my brother again. The three of us then caught the bus to go to the village. I was pleased that we were both going home to the village, even though I did not remember much about it. I enjoyed looking out of the bus window and kept pointing at things and asking questions all the time. Both my *Thea* and Eleftherios kept saying, *"Olympia, ehis fae glistritha?"* (Have you eaten Glistritha?) (Glistritha is a weed which, Greeks believe, makes people talk a lot.)

Baba had been discharged by the army early in 1949. The army, with the help of the English and Americans, had defeated the communist guerrillas. My parents had been working hard to get back on their feet. They appreciated the help that *Mama's* sisters had given them by looking after us for a while. We also had a surprise when we arrived as we found out that we had a younger sister, Anastasia.

Mama was in the middle of harvesting so she had asked her sister, Anna, if she could go to the mill to get the wheat ground as she was out of flour. She needed to bake, but hadn't had time to go to the millers. *Thea* took me with her and it was a wonderful experience to see the wheat become flour. There was flour everywhere in the mill. The miller had flour all over him, and everything was white. I was thrilled to see that and enjoyed the huge water wheel outside the mill with water flowing over it.

I just marvelled at everything and I think the miller had never had anyone telling him how wonderful it was so he decided to give us some of his delicious little apples to take home; the tree was next to the mill near the creek. It had been such a wonderful day for me. On the way home we sang the nursery rhymes that *Thea* taught me and we ate the sweet apples.

My brother had been sent to help *Baba* with the harvest. There was no time to sit and waste time, and we were all given things to do. This was my introduction to village life. I found that we really had to work hard in the village, it did not matter how old you were. My brother was happy that he had some time in Thessaloniki to recover.

Heraklis and Eleftherios both rented *Papou's* house as *Thea* Anna and *Theo* George now owned it. They lived in the house during the week and came home to Tropaioukhos on the weekend. Heraklis went to high school and Eleftherios got his wish to be an apprentice cobbler. But unfortunately he also became the cobbler's babysitter. He looked after their baby and often had to change it as well. He was often asked to do their cooking when they were all busy. He found out that he was not only apprenticed, but he was also a housekeeper to the cobbler. In order to learn the trade he was patient with the cobbler.

Eleftherios loved his apprenticeship even though they had him doing other chores around the home. The cobbler was a good one and he did teach him how to make shoes and repair them. But at the weekends he always came home to work in the fields and help *Mama* and *Baba*. It was wonderful having my brothers at home and I would follow them around. I felt closer to both my brothers than to my parents. Eleftherios would always put me on his shoulder and carry me around.

It was on one of these occasions when I said to him, “Leutheri (that was what I called him), put me down. I need to go to the toilet”.

“No, you can wait till we get home,” said Eleftherios

“Well I need to go NOW. Put me down!” I told him.

“No, you can wait,” he said. I responded with “No, I can’t!” As I had eaten lots of fruit I had diarrhoea and I needed to go to the toilet, but as I was on his shoulders I had an accident, which certainly upset him.

Well, was he mad? He then had to take the back road up to the river. When we got there he threw me in the river then jumped in himself to try to get us both clean. Well, we played and splashed and threw water at each other, and as we laughed and enjoyed the water he yelled at me, “*Skatoula, Skatoula*” (you little shit, you little shit). When we arrived home we both got into trouble as our clothes were wringing wet. We had a special bond; although he was my brother, to me he was also my *Baba* and my friend. Both my brothers were older than me. We had a special bond that was blessed from the caring and sharing of *Papou’s* great love. This special bond lasted all our lives.

#24
VILLAGE LIFE

Summer in the village was a very busy time with the villagers ploughing, planting and harvesting their fields. Each day we started before the crack of dawn. I settled into village life, but soon found out that we all had to work very hard. It did not matter how old you were.

My younger sister Anastasia had been born on 20th of November, 1949 in the hospital at Florina. The godfather Koutsoubithis (the godfather previously mentioned) managed to name her Anastasia, after his daughter who had been killed in the war. Of the four children my parents had, the godfather named three of them with names he selected. I, as mentioned earlier, was named after my maternal grandmother, Olympia. Anastasia was the only child who was with our parents since birth, while my brothers and I had been nurtured, cared for and influenced by our *Papou* Zacharia, then later by our parents.

My sister was younger than me, but she knew the daily routine. She had her chores to do early in the morning of feeding the chickens, ducks and the dogs. Until one morning while feeding the dogs, one of the puppies bit her finger. From then on I had to take over the feeding because she was too scared. Sarko the St. Bernard was tied up in my Giagia Malamati's yard and Lisa the kelpie was in our yard, however, her puppies were very playful and would often chase us and try to bite our heels.

My *Baba* brushed and fed the donkeys, mules, the cow and goats every morning and evening. I loved helping him. He also had two horses the Germans had left behind, one limped and we called him *Koutsaka* ('Limping'). They belonged to my Uncle Parashos Deliyannis, but *Baba* was the only one who would take care of them. We shared these animals as we used them for pulling the ploughs.

Early each morning *Thea* Mersina, who lived next-door, would call out and wake us up so we could go to the fields. "Olga, Giannko, are you up?" (That was the Asia Minor name for *Baba.*) *Baba* harnessed the horses and all of us would climb into the cart with all the gardening tools and seedlings and would head for the fields. On the way we would sing and joke and laugh with each other. While *Baba* ploughed the fields we would clear them of rocks, which were later used for fencing between our fields and those of our neighbours. We also collected any old tree roots for the family fire. The women and children would then follow, planting the tobacco seedlings, corn or wheat. It was very hard work, but everyone helped each other plant first one field and then, one by one, the others.

In the village we lived across the street from the school and the church. On Sunday most women would go to church while the men would usually go to the *Cafenio* where they would play cards, backgammon and drink coffee. If it was a Saint's Day there would be celebrations in the school grounds and dancing and singing with the men, women and children taking part.

One Sunday afternoon the villagers were gathered in the front yard of the school to watch a visiting *Karaztiothis* ('Punch and Judy') show performing in the schoolyard. It was a great treat for the villagers and they all enjoyed the entertainment.

I had seen Punch and Judy in the town a few times, so I volunteered to collect the animals and put them in the barn. However, I found the grey donkey would not budge. It groaned and grunted in the middle of the yard! Suddenly I saw something moving from the back of the donkey. I started screaming at the top of my voice, "*Mama*, *Baba*, come quick! Something is coming out of the donkey's bottom! Oooh... Please hurry, something is coming out of the donkey's bottom".

The villagers stopped watching the Punch and Judy show and began laughing at me. *Baba* came, and helped the donkey deliver its foal. He said to me, "Olympia, each time I see an animal being born I am always excited. It is a miracle. It's just wonderful to see new life. It's God's creation". I watched with my *Baba* as the donkey licked its foal to clean it. I was thrilled to have seen the birth of the foal and I talked about it for days. I loved helping *Baba* clean and feed the animals, especially this little foal.

Everywhere I went I would talk about this little donkey that came out of the bottom of its *Mama* and then she licked it and the little donkey had wobbly legs as it got up. It was so lovely.

I loved having lots of cousins, aunts and uncles in the village and all of them were within walking distance of each other. They were relatives on *Baba's* side and it was always fun when *Mama* would send me on an errand to pick mulberries from *Thea* Taso and *Theo* Thanaso's mulberry tree. They were my favourite aunt and uncle. At times I think *Mama* just wanted to get rid of me. However, I enjoyed playing with my cousins, Stavroulla and Sofie, their daughters, as we climbed the tree and picked and ate the mulberries.

Another special aunt was *Thea* Mersina who lived just across from us. Often I could smell her cooking, especially her lentil soup. I loved to visit her and eat her lovely soup. Of course I told all of them about this little thing that came out of the donkey's bottom, which was a baby donkey, and just how beautiful it was. And that *Baba* let me brush it in the evening and he felt so soft.

Mama would reprimand me, "Olympia, Olympia, your *Thea* Mersina has an army to feed (she had eight children) and you burden her by staying and having a meal there". I would argue with *Mama,* "*Thea* Mersina doesn't mind me staying. She likes me, *Mama*".

Whenever we harvested the corn, in the evening we would all sit around a bonfire, cleaning it. The older people would tell stories and jokes, which I loved, listening to and joining in the laughter and sharing. There were my *Theo* Christopher, his wife Ourania, my cousin Anna, my grandma Malamati, *Thea* Mersina and her children.

I loved it when *Baba* would bring home the full tobacco baskets from the field as he always had a little present for me. He would say, "I wonder what is in here?" and look through the tobacco and bring out a little round watermelon and give it to me. It was always sweet and juicy. In the evening we would all sit around and thread the tobacco. Young and old had to thread a needle through the tobacco leaves and our fingers got very sticky. After a while my fingers hurt badly. We all threaded the tobacco by hand in those days and then *Baba* would hang the threaded tobacco on wooden frames he had made to dry.

A most wonderful time I remember was when the family picked the grapes and made wine in a large timber barrel. All the grapes went into a huge barrel and Theo Christopher, *Baba*, Heraklis and Eleftherios were all dancing and singing as they squashed the grapes with their feet. As the juice came through a tap *Mama*, Grandmother Malamati and *Thea* Ourania would pour it into smaller barrels.

I wanted so much to join in the fun, but *Mama* would not let me. I pleaded and pleaded. "*Mama*, please can I help and dance in the barrel too?"

"Olympia, stop it! Little girls do not go jumping on the grapes in the wine press."

I really could not understand why I could not help in crushing the grapes since they all seemed to be having such a wonderful time. It was a very big disappointment for me.

Making wine, pickles, preserves and jams during summer was a busy time for all the families. *Mama* had handpicked a bucket of large strawberries and she was going to make *gliko* (jam) with them. They had a big order of strawberries to pick for the markets, so *Mama* left my sister and me in the house while the rest of the family went at dawn to pick the strawberries. *Mama* had all the fruit and the sugar ready so that she could cook the jam when she came home. I said to my sister, "Tasoula, (that was what I called my sister as I could not say Anastasia), I think we should help our *Mama* and cook this strawberry jam". So the two of us sat and squashed all the strawberries in the bucket with our little hands then added the sugar. Unfortunately strawberries ended up all over the floor, on our clothes, in our hair, our face, everywhere. When *Mama* walked into the house she was very upset with what she saw and yelled at me, "Olympia, what have you done?"

"*Mama*, I wanted to help you make the jam," I told her.

"Olympia, take your sister and go and wash her at the tap and wash yourself and here is a bucket. Fill this up with water so that we can clean all this mess. I just don't want to see either of you. Do you hear me? Go! And do not be too long, do you hear." She was extremely upset.

So I took my sister's hand and the bucket and we went to the communal tap. Oh me, oh my, what a wonderful time we had at the trough, splashing and playing with the water. It was great fun. Suddenly a shepherd came along and yelled at us for dirtying the water. He chased us away with the crook he had in his hand. He had brought all his animals to drink from the trough. He was a very big man with a large, round face that was really red and he had huge eyes. Thinking back I would say his face was well burnt by the sun and wind. He wore a heavy black cloak over his shoulder and he had a very loud voice as he yelled at us.

I was not impressed, but then when we went home *Mama* spanked me for getting all wet, and forgetting the bucket at the tap and for spoiling her jam-making. She ordered "Olympia, go and get changed and help your sister to change her clothes too".

"Yes *Mama*," I mumbled.

After I had changed, *Mama* said, "Olympia, take your *Baba's* lunch to him. He is picking strawberries in the paddocks".

"All right, *Mama,*" I replied. She gave me a container with a handle on it to take to him. It had *Baba's* bean soup in it.

I was carrying this container with the hot food when every now and then my legs would get burnt as the container touched them. I carried it for a while until I saw some children playing marbles. I was curious so I put the container down on the side of the road and watched for a while. "Can I play marbles with you?" I asked them. "Sure, you can join us," they said. They lent me some of their marbles and showed me how to play the game. It was really great fun; we were all having a wonderful time. But I forgot all about *Baba's* lunch, didn't I? I was having such a wonderful time until *Mama* come along as she was heading for the fields to help *Baba*. She saw me and then *Baba's* lunch by the side of the road. She was very angry and started yelling at me. I was not very popular. Well, did I get into trouble?

"Olympia, you naughty girl! Your *Baba* is hungry and he is waiting for his lunch and you are here playing marbles." She grabbed me and then spanked me really hard on my bottom. My pride was hurt more than the spanking as the other children glared at me. I was not impressed with *Mama* and I told her so. "I don't like you. You're not my *Mama*, my *Thea* Anna is. I want to go back to *Thea* Anna. I hate you!"

"Do you now!" *Mama* was so furious she spanked me again and again and then pulled me along with her as she carried *Baba's* lunch.

In the strawberry paddock she said to me, "Now, young lady I want you to pick strawberries while your *Baba* has his lunch, and no more cheek from you. Here is your basket. Do you hear me?"

"Yes, *Mama,*" I grumbled. But I was not very happy about it. I was annoyed as all I seemed to do was to get into trouble. Picking strawberries is hard work, as you bend all the time, and I had to keep filling my little basket with strawberries continuously. But *Baba* was proud of me as he said to me, "Olympia, you are doing a great job, keep up the good work". And he winked at me. From then on I felt I liked *Baba* better than my *Mama*.

#25
Commencing school

For my first day at school, *Mama* had made me the school uniform, which was like a blue overshirt. I had brand-new shoes to wear. *Mama* dressed me and put a white bow in my hair. She loved bows and would take time combing my hair and then tying the bow on my head. I, in fact, hated the bow, so as soon she was not looking I would pull it off and throw it away. She could not understand how my sister's bow stayed on her hair all day while mine just got lost.

The school was across the road from our house so I just walked across when the bell went. All the children would line up outside and then our teacher would take us to our classroom. It was a spacious room with a combustion stove at one corner to keep the room warm in winter. Each student had to supply wood for that stove. There was a large blackboard at the front and the teacher had her table and chair between the blackboard and the students' desks. We had the desks facing the blackboard and large windows on one side. The teacher was a skinny lady with a gentle voice who I did enjoy listening to when she told us stories or taught us the many nursery rhymes.

I enjoyed school and found that I knew a lot of the nursery rhymes that were being taught as my *Thea* Anna had already taught them to me. The teacher was patient and loved her students. She also showed dedication by persevering to help some of us, who spoke different dialects, to learn to read and write. My friend with whom I sat, and often talked to, was Kostandina. Many times we would giggle and talk, but because we talked so much we often got into trouble. Her father had a business roasting chick peas. Each time I visited her home I would take home a bag of freshly roasted chick peas, which I loved to eat.

When I visited her home we watched the ovens while her father roasted the chick peas as we were both very curious. We were often told not to go too close to the ovens. One day I found that Kostandina was not at school and I was really worried as she and I never missed a day at school. Neither of us ever seemed to get sick even though it was very cold. Winter was approaching fast and we had snow in the highlands. We knew we would soon have snow in the village.

"*Mama*, Kostandina has not been at school for a few days. Something is wrong because she is always at school and I have had to sit by myself. Can we please visit her and also buy some more chick peas, please, *Mama*?" *Mama* was always so busy it was hard for her to take time out. But she came with me, so for a change it was good to have her to myself. We left my sister at my grandmother's place and we strolled together to pay a visit to my friend's home. *Mama* and I walked to their house; it was good to be with *Mama* and as she held my hand I skipped along beside her as she said, "Olympia can't you be still for once? Do you always have to be jumping up and down?"

I giggled as I enjoyed being alone with *Mama* for a while.

When we reached my friend's place I could not smell the usual aroma of roasted chick peas. It was all very quiet and strange. There was not the usual hustle and bustle of customers coming and going. They let us in and were very pleased we had come.

Mrs Stragallou said "Thank you for coming; we really appreciate you visiting us."

"Olympia said that Kostandina had not been at school for a few days so she was concerned that she may be sick," *Mama* replied.

"Come and see for yourselves. There has been an accident and we nearly lost Kostandina. But thank God she will pull through, but it will be a while before she goes back to school again."

We entered the living room and Kostandina was lying on a flat mattress on the floor with a white sheet over her. Only her face was showing. I went over to her and kneeled close and said, "Kostandina, I've missed you not being at school. Are you all right?"

"Olympia, thank you for coming. I have missed you too, but I cannot move as all the front of me is burnt," Kostandina said.

"Kostandina, tell Olympia what you did," Mrs Stragallou said.

"Olympia, I was naughty. I wanted to help my father roast the chick peas. I opened the oven and was playing with the fire when all the coals fell on me. My clothes were on fire and my father come racing in when he heard my screams and threw a blanket over me to stop the fire, but now I cannot move as I am hurting lots all over," Kostandina explained, while tears were running down her face as she was in so much pain.

Mrs Stragallou continued, "We have been at the hospital in Florina and the doctors have done the best they can. We know it will just take time before she is well. But *Doxa to Theo* (thank God) as it could have been a lot worse".

While *Mama* and the rest of the family were having a cup of coffee I sat with Kostandina and put my hand over her head and said to her, "I will pray for you and you will get better. That is what *Papou* used to do".

Kostandina's parents were friendly with my *Mama* and she enjoyed their company. They appreciated us visiting her, but it took a long time before she went back to school. Ever since then I was very careful when the fire was on as I remembered it had taken my friend such a long time to recover.

#26

APPENDICITIS

Christmas was approaching fast, and at school we were learning Christmas carols. I was so pleased and loved singing just as long as I had an audience. *Mama* sent my sister and me to my godparents' home to sing Christmas carols to them. Holding Tasoula's hand we headed for their house, which was not too far from our home.

I knocked on their door and my godmother opened it. Well, I was so happy I started with a few carols and then had to sing all of them. My godparents blessed us and filled our little bags with goodies, walnuts, sultanas and fruit.

By late that afternoon I felt really sick. "*Mama,* I don't feel well, I have a pain in my stomach."

"You have eaten too much again," she replied as she tucked me into bed.

The next morning *Baba* woke everyone up as he yelled, "Come quickly. The first snow has arrived; we will have a white Christmas". *Baba* then had to go out and clear the snow from our front door.

We all ran outside and threw snowballs at each other, then with my brothers and my sister we built a beautiful snowman. It was so much fun.

I then followed *Baba* to help him feed the animals and clean the barn at *Giagia's* house, but I was in pain again and I doubled up and cried out "My stomach hurts".

Giagia (Malamati) was close by and heard me and yelled at my *Baba*, "Giannko, this child is sick; take her home now".

"*Manna,* Olympia was playing in the snow all day. She must have caught a cold. Don't worry, she will be all right."

Malamati took my little hand and said, "I will take her home, Giannko. This child is burning".

"I'll be home in a little while. I only have the pigs to feed. Tell Olga to serve dinner as I won't be long."

I doubled up in pain and could not walk. *Giagia* picked me up and headed to our place. By the time we got home I was really hot. My temperature had gone up and I was crying. *Mama* and *Giagia* had never seen me like that before.

They both decided that I must have caught a cold. So they covered me well so that I could sweat the cold out. *Giagia* heated a brick, wrapped it in tea towel and gently placed it on my stomach.

My nose started bleeding badly and I tossed and turned trying to throw the covers off while they tried to keep the covers on me.

"The child is dying!" Malamati shouted.

"No, she is not!" yelled *Mama*. "Go away, she will be fine. She only has a cold."

"Yes, she is. My daughter Despina was hot like that before she died," Malamati muttered, while tears were running down her face as she held my hand tightly.

"*Manna*, go and call Giannko. We will take Olympia to the doctor. Go quickly!" my *Mama* told her.

As Malamati raced out the door she noticed the old black car that belonged to the doctor parked in the street. She ran as fast as her legs would carry her calling out, "Doctor! Doctor! My granddaughter is dying. Come quickly!"

The doctor was visiting a neighbouring village and was driving through Tropaioukhos but had stopped to talk to some locals.

When the doctor examined me he said, "You are killing this child with the hot brick. Uncover her quickly, we need to bring her temperature down. She has acute appendicitis. She must be taken to the hospital immediately. Pack her bag and yours and come with me".

Mama packed quickly and taking me in her arms got into the doctor's car.

Everyone waved at us as my *Mama* and I headed for the hospital in Florina.

Giagia prayed *'O God, don't let her die'*. *Baba's* face was so sad as they all waved at us. *Baba* kept on praying *'o Christos nika ta panda'* (Christ conquers all).

The doctor at Florina Hospital would not touch me. "She is dying. I cannot operate on her as her appendix has burst," he told *Mama*.

Mama pleaded, "Please, doctor, you cannot give up".

"The best thing you can do is take her to Thessaloniki. The hospital there is large and has surgeons who are both specialised and experienced," he replied, his face ashen with grave concern, as he didn't think I would make it. He knew that the bus took three hours to travel from Florina to Thessaloniki.

I don't remember much of the bus ride to Thessaoniki's main hospital where I was operated on, and because my appendix had burst it was removed and the area thoroughly cleaned. I was very sick and the doctors prepared *Mama* for the worst possible outcome. I had been unconscious for many days and *Mama* was by my bedside for the whole time, praying that I would live. Christmas had come and gone, but there were no celebrations in the family.

I awoke and saw *Mama* sitting in a chair beside the bed. I said, "*Mama*, are you all right?" She looked so tired and worn out.

"Olympia! Olympia, my child, you are awake. You are going to live! Thank God you are all right. Doctor! Doctor!" she called out and the nurse came racing in. *Mama* was so excited and happy.

"*Mama,* where are we?" I looked around. Everything was so white. I had never been in such a white place. I was really puzzled.

"You are in the hospital, Olympia. You had a big operation," replied my *Mama*.

Mama was so thrilled as many people those days had died from a burst appendix. She was so thankful to God that she kept on thanking Him.

The doctor came and checked me out, and asked how I felt,

"Olympia, how do you feel?"

"I feel tired," I replied as I tried to lift my head to see *Mama* and it was difficult to do that.

"That's all right, it will take time, young lady, but slowly you will feel better. Just take it easy as you frightened all of us."

"Yes, Doctor," I mumbled and dropped off to sleep again.

When I woke up again I felt a lot better and *Mama* was excited and asked me "Olympia, what would you like me to get you?"

For the first time in my life I didn't ask for food, but I asked for a toy.

"*Mama*, can I have a big bus?"

Mama and *Thea* Sapfo went shopping and bought me a beautiful red bus with a little doll driver.

"Oh *Mama*! It is so lovely! Thank you! Thank you ever so much." It was the very first toy I had ever owned.

I stayed in the hospital for a while. The doctor was so funny as he kept on coming and asking me if I had farted. He said to me, "Olympia, you will leave the hospital only if you fart". Then one day as I was lying in bed I suddenly did fart. They all asked if it was me, as there was another young lady in the other bed beside me who had had her appendix out. She had been pregnant, but had lost her baby due to her burst appendix.

At the top of my voice I yelled out "I did" and they all burst out laughing.

The doctor then allowed me to go but warned *Mama* "She must be very careful, make sure she doesn't run or jump for a while."

Mama and I stayed in Thessaloniki with my *Thea* Sapfo and *Theo* George and their two children, Spiro and Kosta, until I was well enough to travel back to Tropaioukhos.

I loved my cousins and it was great to play with them. My cousin had a tricycle and I constantly wanted to ride it. I had never seen a tricycle before! It was a great experience for me.

#27

Lost in Thessaloniki

I enjoyed the time with my *Thea*, *Theo* and cousins. *Thea* Sapfo often sent Spiro to the local shop to buy bread or milk and newspapers and I always demanded to go as well. I wanted to go and help so I kept annoying him with, "Spiro, please let me go and help you. I am all right now, I can walk".

One day *Mama* and *Thea* had a visitor and, while they were having a cup of coffee, they sent Spiro to buy bread and milk and finally I was allowed to go to the shop with him. I was very excited and in awe of all the traffic.

"What's wrong with you? Close your mouth, Olympia," Spiro said to me.

"There are so many people and cars! And what's that? It looks like a bus with poles sticking out," I asked.

"Stupid, it's a tram! My *Baba* drives one of them," Spiro said proudly.

"Isn't he smart? There are so many people on them. Gee, I really would like to go on a tram one day."

"I have ridden on trams many times," Spiro said, feeling important. "When *Baba* comes home I will ask him to take us for a ride," Spiro said, being very proud of his *Baba*.

At the shop Spiro instructed me, "Olympia, just wait outside. I am only buying bread and milk".

I was fascinated with the city life, the trolley buses, the trams, all the traffic and noise and especially the tall buildings. I wandered off admiring everything. I had never been to a big city before and could not believe the huge number of people who were here in Thessaloniki. I was just amazed. My eyes were wide open and I stared and wandered away from the shop. I was enjoying the city sights as if I was in wonderland.

Hours later when I started feeling hungry I realised that I didn't know where I was or anyone I could talk to. I was lost in this huge city. I kept looking around to see if I could remember *Thea's* house, but they all looked the same, just tall buildings with people going in and out.

I felt there was a man following me for a while. I just had this feeling he was behind me and I did not feel good about it. As I crossed street after street I was pretending I knew where I was going, but I was going nowhere. Then I came to a very busy intersection. There were many people waiting to cross the street. I noticed the man in the centre who was wearing a uniform and directing the traffic. I thought yes, he must be a policeman as *Theo* George in Kastoria wore a uniform and my *Theo* George, Spiro's *Baba*, also wore a uniform. He must know my uncles. With no road sense I ran across to him. Cars screeched to a halt and people screamed at me.

I reached the policeman and grabbed his legs (as he was very tall) and said, "Please, could you take me to my *Theo* George".

"Saint George is surely looking after you!" And he crossed himself in amazement. "It's a miracle you are still alive. Don't you ever cross the road like that again, young lady!" the astounded policeman reprimanded me.

"Just stay where you are. Do not move and then we will go and find your *Theo* George," the policeman said. He continued directing the traffic for a while. I just did not budge. I stood right next to him and watched all the people and cars.

When he finished he took my hand and said to me, "Now, young lady, when you cross the street look to the left and then to the right and then to the left and, if nothing is coming, you can cross the road. Do you hear me?"

He held my hand and we crossed the road and went to his car. It was a big black one. I was thrilled sitting next to him. He drove us to the police station. He handed me to another policeman and there were other policemen there. I entertained them all by singing all the nursery rhymes and told them about the donkey and the little donkey that come out of its bottom and Lisa our dog, which had puppies, and they all had a laugh.

Then one of them brought me an ice-cream, and said "This is for you Olympia."

I had never eaten one. "What is it?" I asked.

"You haven't tasted an ice cream?" he asked very surprised.

"No!"

"Then lick it and see if you like it." The young policeman said this with a grin on his face. I slowly licked it and then I licked it again.

"It is so sweet and cold, I love it," I exclaimed, and then enjoyed the rest of it. (I was hooked on ice-creams from then on.)

They asked me lots of questions and I told them my name and that I came from Tropaioukhos with my *Mama*. But we were staying with my *Theo* and *Thea* as I had been sick and had to get better. I had been in hospital for a long time. Then I showed them the big scar on my tummy. I told them, "My *Theo* George drives a tram. My cousin Spiro told me that one day my *Theo* will take me for a ride on the tram". I was very proud of my *Theo*.

"Would you like to go to see your *Theo* George in the trams Olympia?" the young policeman asked me.

"Yes, please" I said excitedly.

He took my hand and we headed outside where he put me in the sidecar of a motorbike and then climbed on to the bike himself. An older policeman came running out with my *Thea* Sapfo behind him. She yelled, "Olympia! Olympia, my sweet, you are all right! Thank God". She then crossed herself thankfully. She was so relieved that I had been found she was crying with happiness.

"I am so pleased you found my niece," she said to the policemen.

"Well actually Olympia found us," the older policeman said.

Thea went to pick me up, "No, *Thea*, I am going for a ride with this nice policeman to *Theo* George's tram," I told her firmly. "Young lady, you have worried all of us. You have been naughty, you are going home with me now. Do you hear me?" my *Thea* yelled at me.

The young officer said, "Come on, I will take you both home and Olympia can have her ride on the motorbike".

Thea Sapfo was angry and said, "But officer, you are too busy. We don't want to trouble you".

"It is no trouble, I am on my way home as it is," he replied.

My *Thea* squashed into the sidecar holding me. I had the biggest grin on my face as I enjoyed the ride and the wind blowing on my face. I yelled out with excitement, "This is wonderful!"

Thea was fuming as her hair was windblown. She always liked her hair to be tidy.

The policeman stopped in front of *Thea's* house and took me out and then helped *Thea* out of the sidecar.

"Thank you, officer," she said, and then grabbed me and stomped into her home furiously.

My *Thea* was windblown and annoyed with me when we got in. *Mama* was waiting anxiously. When we walked in she grabbed me from Sapfo's arms as she said "Olympia! Olympia! Where have you been? We have been so worried!"

"*Mama*, I had such a wonderful time. I saw lots of things. I ate an ice-cream and I had a ride in a police car and on a motorbike. Oh it was fun," I said excitedly.

"What?" *Mama* said, looking at her sister with a puzzled look. Sapfo's face was very pale and her hair untidy. "Sapfo, are you all right?" *Mama* asked her sister.

"I am angry. I am annoyed. I cannot believe your daughter. She is incredible. She refused to leave unless she had a ride on the motorbike. I am windblown, my hair is in a mess and the young police officer insisted he bring us home in his stupid bike. I froze to death with the wind blowing on my face. I need to warm up," my *Thea* complained.

"Sapfo, do you remember we have to visit our great-*Thea*. She wants to see Olympia as Olympia has her sister's name, and she is dying. This morning our cousin who visited us said she did not have long to live and she has been asking for Olympia."

"Oh yes I forgot about that, Olga. Please make me a cup of coffee while I go and brush my hair and tidy myself, then I might feel better".

#28

My Great-Aunt's blessing

Thea and *Mama* refreshed themselves, changed into warmer clothes and waited for *Theo* George to come home. After our evening meal we left *Theo* to look after the boys. He said, "It is cold out there; *Varthari* has been blowing all day today. The wind is certainly cold and has come up suddenly and it's blowing through like cutting ice. It is certainly fierce out there tonight". (Thessaloniki was famous for its cold wind, known as Varthari.)

"Tell me about it!" said Sapfo. "It was freezing when I was on the motorbike".

"What do you mean, *koukla mou* (my doll)?" asked George, who had not been told about their day's experience.

"I'll explain later. I'm in a hurry," she said as they took their coats from the hook in the hallway.

We caught a tram. I was thrilled and sat between *Mama* and *Thea* Sapfo as I watched everyone coming and going. We went to an outer suburb of Thessaloniki. From the tram stop we walked to a rambling old house and went up a flight of narrow stairs into a big, dark room. Heavy, velvet red curtains covered the windows and darkened the room as my great-*Thea* was lying there on a big old four-poster bed. I had never seen such a big bed. In one corner of the room there was an *iconostassi* (a group of religious icons) and a candle was burning in the middle of them.

Mama and *Thea* bent down and kissed their *Thea* and they held her hand as they said to her, "*Thea,* we have brought Olympia to see you. Anna your daughter had told us that you have been asking for Olympia. She is the only one that is carrying the family Christian name."

"Let me see the child. Let me see Olympiatha, let me bless her. And thank God our family name will continue." *Mama* put me on the bed close to the old *Thea,* who looked at me and said, "H Dunami *TouTheou Na ine pandode mazi sou Olympiatha (May God's Strength be always with you Olympiatha)*. It belonged to your great-grandmother. My grandmother came from Olympia, she was a child bride and betrothed to a man in Thrace she had never seen. When they had their first granddaughter she named her Olympia to remind her of her birthplace the city of Olympia. It was a place she loved, but she never set eyes on it again. Her dying wish had been that every first granddaughter born in the family must carry the name. Whoever carried the name must carry it with pride and dignity or a curse would be put on the family that did not continue with the name".

The city of Olympia had a proud tradition. It brought countries together every four years in a friendly competition in peace and harmony, the original Olympic Games. This was to show people the glory of human achievement. Regardless of their fighting and arguments, the City-states of Greece would come together every four years at Olympia to compete against each other in a range of sports in a spirit of friendship and sportsmanship.

The Olympic Games were first celebrated in Olympia in 776BC and continued until abolished by the Roman Emperor Theodosius 1 in 393AD after Greece had been occupied by the Romans.

The modern Olympics were commenced in 1896, under the patronage of the King of Greece, when a new stadium was built in Athens.

To me that blessing did not mean anything at the time. I just enjoyed the attention and the soft bed that I found. It was great to bounce on it as I had never seen anything like it before. *Mama* reprimanded me.

"Olympia, can't you keep still for a change?" as she grabbed me off the bed so that I would not disturb my great *Thea*.

"Leave her. She is certainly a live one. It's good to see spirit in a child," my great-*Thea* said.

"She certainly has the spirit, she is a live one. She just does not stop," my *Thea* Sapfo said.

We all sat quietly next to the bed, and *Mama* held me tightly so that I did not disturb the old lady. My *Thea* Sapfo held *Thea's* hand and prayed softly. We left her as she had fallen asleep and we headed home. The great-*Thea* died peacefully in her sleep that night. The funeral was held two days later and then *Mama* and I travelled back home to Tropaioukhos.

Those events to a child were not very important at the time. I have found that the older I get the meaning of the blessings for me are very significant. I feel this is the heritage or legacy that I can leave for my grandchildren to show them their family tree and their heritage.

#29
Easter in the Village

Mama and I returned to Tropaioukhos by bus. The snow was melting and the villagers were happy to see the sun shining after their cold, miserable winter. In winter they were often housebound for weeks because of the heavy snow. During this time when they could not work in the fields, the men occupied themselves by feeding and cleaning the animals or spending time at the *cafenion* discussing politics, playing cards or backgammon.

They would weave baskets, which they used to collect and carry strawberries, tobacco leaves and other vegetables. The women knitted, embroidered, crocheted or weaved blankets and rugs.

With the warmer weather it was a very busy time. The women would spring-clean and put all of their bedding out in the sun to air. They whitewashed their houses and planted geraniums in their window boxes. It was always a challenge between *Mama* and my *Theas* to see who would have the best windowsill display for summer.

Swallows were returning to build their nests, and the villagers were preparing their fields for summer. The grapevines and the fruit trees had been pruned and the first buds were now appearing on the fruit trees. The yellow daffodils, lilac irises, yellow daisies and red poppies were flowering in the fields as spring was in the air.

Easter arrived early that year. Jesus' resurrection and the new life of nature were all around. Easter was a great celebration with all of us helping *Mama* with dyeing the eggs red and decorating them with patterns. Holy Thursday is a wonderful celebration throughout Greece with all the families in each home dyeing their eggs red, the color of Christ's blood. I loved helping my *Mama* bake the Greek Easter buns (which I still bake each Easter). They were made with lots of eggs, yeast, orange peel, sugar, butter, flour and milk, and the aniseed was boiled very slowly and then put in the mixture. That was the great secret in *Mama's* beautiful Easter buns. *Mama* would knead the dough and then wait until it rose, then she would knead it again before forming all the beautiful buns. On the top of each bun a red egg was placed in the centre and *Mama* would let me glaze them. While this was going on, *Baba* prepared the old brick oven outside until it was really hot. When it was hot enough *Mama* would put the buns in to bake and the smell was wonderful. She would always place a few quinces in the oven in between the buns and the aroma of all that baking was just marvellous.

We would all have to fast for a few weeks before Easter so that we could then go to Church and receive our communion. That meant no meat, chicken, milk, eggs or animal products; our diet would simply be a vegetarian one.

On Easter Saturday, everyone attended midnight Mass. The church was packed as all came to celebrate Christ's Resurrection. Everyone carried with them their red or decorated eggs to crack and Easter candles to light.

I have such wonderful memories of the first Easter that I still remember. We all went to sleep early on the Saturday night and then *Baba* would wake us up at 11 o'clock so we could attend midnight Mass.

"Olympia, Tasoula, wake up, we are going to church," he said and he handed us each a tiny basket that was made from wax-coated twine. The twine was actually a candle to light for midnight Mass. Inside this basket he placed a red egg. It was just beautiful.

"Olympia, Tasoula, don't break your eggs until the priest tells us that Christ is risen. And do not eat them! Do you hear me?" *Mama* told us.

"Yes, *Mama*," we said, half asleep. My brothers then helped my sister Tasoula and I get dressed in the new dresses *Mama* had made for us. I had a red one and Tasoula had a blue one. We both had our hair combed and, to my horror, a big white bow was placed on our heads.

All the family was dressed in their best clothes as we went to midnight Mass. We would also take our communion after fasting for days and we would be allowed to eat meat again.

At exactly midnight the lights were turned off in the little packed church and the priest announced, *"Christos Anesti"* (Christ is risen.)

The congregation responded, in unison *"Alithos Anseti"* (He is risen indeed).

The priest then lit his candle, followed by the entire congregation who lit theirs. At that point they broke their eggs with each other. Each person held their eggs and said, *"Christos Anesti"*. (Christ is risen.) A second person would crack the other person's egg with theirs and say *"Alithos Anesti"* (He is risen indeed) to symbolise the new life.

After the midnight Mass we walked home. We all sat down to a meal of an egg and lemon soup that my *Mama* had simmering on the stove. We broke eggs with each other and enjoyed our Easter buns.

On Easter Sunday all the families and friends came together to celebrate; it was the time for rejoicing that Jesus had risen. They would roast lambs on spits in their back yards. They cracked their red eggs and shared their meals and their Easter buns ending their fasting, as they had taken their communion at midnight Mass. This was to celebrate Jesus' resurrection and the new life of spring. The delicious smells and aromas in the area were just tantalising. I loved the wonderful Easter food, especially the buns, and the family sharing, upholding, renewing and encouraging each other as my parents were thankful to God for what we shared.

Mama gave thanks to God for the food and the family and then she announced, "Heraklis' papers have come through. He is migrating to Australia and soon he will be leaving us". Heraklis was very happy as at the age of 19 he would have far more opportunities in Australia than in Greece. He had finished high school, but there was no work for him and many others his age were leaving the country for a better life. My parents did not have the money to send him for a higher education, so there was only one option, he had to migrate for a better life and to help the family.

Heraklis had applied to go to Canada. That was his first choice as his godfather was in Canada. But his second choice, Australia, had come through. My brother was very happy and excited. However, *Mama* was very upset as she was losing her eldest son. She wondered how he would cope on his own in the new country.

#30
HERAKLIS' FAREWELL PARTY

Mama wanted to send Heraklis off with a farewell party so that he could have fond memories of the family and friends. She had been preparing food for days and kept us all busy as we had to help her with the cooking and the cleaning of the house.

The family, relatives and friends came from everywhere. *Thea* Giannoula with her daughter, Berberka, her son Thomas, and her grandson, Gianni came from Florina. *Thea* Sapfo and her sons, Spiros and Kostas, travelled from Thessaloniki. *Thea* Anna and *Theo* George came from Kastoria with their baby, Zacharia. The relatives from around the neighbourhood, *Giagia* Malamati, *Theo* Christopher, *Thea* Ourania and their children, Anna, Thanasis and Arhodoula, *Thea* Mersine and *Thea* Parasho and their children all came. *Thea* Taso and *Theo* Thanasos and their children, Stavroula, Sofoula and Chris, arrived.

Mama worked hard baking and cooking for days for the guests. There were no such things as balloons or streamers, but there was a huge amount of food, pitas, meatballs, souvlakia, stuffed vegetables, stuffed vine leaves, pickles and salads. For desserts *Mama* made halva, honey puffs, *melines* (pita bread), shortbread cookies and a big batch of fresh bread. It was the very first time I had seen so much food.

There was dancing and singing as we had *Theo* playing the fiddle. I had never seen so many people in our home before. *Baba* had an old stove downstairs in the cellar that was used to heat the food, but that meant they had to use the stepladder each time to take the food down, heat it then bring it back up, as we still only had two rooms finished and the living area was upstairs. There were people singing and dancing and drinking and laughing. This was the very first party that I can remember. It was a wonderful experience.

Unfortunately as my cousin, Berberka was bringing food up the ladder she missed her footing and she fell back down. My parents were really concerned thinking that she may have broken her legs or hurt her back, but thank God she was all right.

The celebrations went on all night and we then all collapsed early in the morning on the rugs and blankets that *Mama* had placed on the floor for all to sleep and rest. We all laughed, joked and giggled as we laid there. I tried to keep awake as it was all very exciting to have so many people in our place all at once, but I soon fell asleep with all the other young ones.

We were all woken up with *Mama* and the *Theas* cooking *melines. Mama* would put flour and oil in a big bowl and then slowly add the water and a pinch of salt and then knead this and make firm, round balls of dough. Then she flattened each one and put it into the frying pan, first to cook it on one side and then flip it over and cook it on the other side. Our breakfast was the fresh *melines* that some had with fetta cheese, olives or strawberry jam with hot coffee.

Our relatives and friends all hugged and cried as they said their goodbyes to my brother and wished him all the best for his trip. That weekend we all had a little rest from our usual chores, but we knew we would have to catch up on Monday with the ploughing and planting.

As usual our *Thea* Mersine woke us up early the next day by her usual call. It was still dark as she yelled at the top of her voice, "Olga,

Giannko, are you up?" Her call was always followed by her banging on the door, making sure all of us were awake.

Baba was up to light the kerosene lamp for light and the combustion stove to heat the house and for cooking. When we got up, there was either haricot bean soup or lentil soup cooking slowly on the stove. The aroma was delicious as *Mama* added lots of herbs and vegetables to these soups. We did not have meat. There was only the occasional chicken or fish in our diet; it was mainly a vegetarian diet. *Mama* would soak the beans overnight and in the morning she would rinse them well, then cut onions and garlic and fry that in some oil in a big pot. She would then add the beans, stir that with lots of herbs and lots of paprika then add the homemade salsa and salt, pepper, carrots and celery. Water was added and then cooked very slowly for our dinner. *Mama* would make a big batch of tomato salsa each summer, which was used for cooking throughout the year. I remembered her having a huge boiler outside on four bricks with a fire going underneath. With the fresh tomato salsa cooking and bubbling out in the open the aroma was wonderful. When it was cooked I loved her putting salsa on a piece of fresh, crusty bread she had baked in the outside mud-brick oven that morning. The salsa had lots of herbs and eating it was delicious. At times *Mama* would put either apples or quinces in the hot coals once the bread had been baked and they just smelt amazing while they were baking. That was *Mama's* treat for us, baked apples or quinces.

Baba and Heraklis went to the barn to get the cart, tools and the seedlings. While one harnessed the bullock team to the wagon the other put all the tools into the cart and always put the large kerosene lamp on the cart.

Mama finished making dinner and then prepared our lunch to take with us to the fields. This usually consisted of bread up to seven days old (as baking was only done once a week), feta cheese, olives and possibly some spring onions, and a jug of water from the spring. Eleftherios would help Tasoula and me to get dressed; this was our daily ritual.

All of our family would climb into the cart. *Thea* Mersine and her children, Fanakos, Elizabeth and Dimitri, usually travelled with us; *Theo*

Parashos would come later to do their ploughing. Only the younger ones helped *Thea* Mersine as the two oldest girls, Anastasia and Chrissi, were seamstresses and worked hard to help the family financially, while Kuriako was a high school teacher and the other two, George and Pluto, went to high school in Florina and could only help at weekends or summer holidays. All of us together with the gardening tools and the seedlings headed for our fields. As it was still dark, we held old kerosene lamps to light our way. More wagons joined along the way as each family travelled to the fields.

There were fields for tobacco, vegetables, wheat and strawberries, and as these fields were not all in the one area they had to work out where they had to go to plough and plant at different times. Each household had adjoining fields for the different crops. If tobacco was to be planted, they would all work on that. If it was wheat, again they each would assist with planting and harvesting.

These fields had been allocated when the exchange had taken place between Turkey and Greece so that they had enough to feed themselves. There was one area where they all grew wheat; another was for tobacco and in another area, corn. But although these fields had been (supposedly) allocated freely when they got married the villagers found out later that they still had to pay for them.

Even though they all worked hard to just make a living they were happy and made the best of what they had. They sang, joked and laughed on the way to the fields. They all supported each other. By sharing they were able to support and care for one another.

"Heraklis! Heraklis! Ahh *Manam*… it is your last day today. You must be very excited, migrating to Australia" said *Thea* Mersine.

"I am excited, *Thea* Mersine, but sad as well for leaving all of you behind," replied Heraklis.

"Yes, *Thea* Mersine, he is sad because he will miss your wake-up call" Eleftherios added. We all laughed, except *Mama* and *Baba*. They were quiet. Their eldest son was leaving. While the others laughed and joked, their hearts ached. *Mama* prayed silently that God would always help

Heraklis' path. She knew that she had to let go. Hopefully, whatever he faced in the future would make him a strong and better man.

"Who is going to wake you up from now on?" I asked, as I was concerned about Heraklis.

"Oh he will find a young wife to look after him and wake him up, don't worry about him," *Thea* Mersine retorted.

"I have seen in magazines clocks you can set up to ring to wake you up," Heraklis countered.

"I would like to see a clock like that," I said, very puzzled.

"I hope you won't forget us, as you become rich and have lots of money and lots of girlfriends, a handsome young man like you. And you won't forget to send us a letter now and then? Remember us as we slave in this poor and harsh land," *Thea* Mersine requested, hopefully.

"Another busload of people is leaving this afternoon," Eleftherios said.

"Yes. Each household can feel the pain of losing a loved one; one by one the young people are leaving the village," *Mama* said.

"Our village will be empty the way things are going," said *Thea* Mersine.

"We are going because there are no jobs around and no opportunities here. We want to better ourselves, *Thea* Mersine," Heraklis said.

We all worked before stopping to have breakfast. We had the crusty bread, some olives and cheese and washed it down with cold water from the spring. The water was in a pottery jug. While having breakfast Heraklis asked *Mama,* "Is it all right to go and say goodbye to some of my friends as we have organised a game of football in the field, before I leave this afternoon."

"Yes, that's fine but take your sisters with you," *Mama* said.

He took Tasoula and me along and we watched as Heraklis and his mates played a last game of football with some friends.

Some of his friends had arrived from Florina. They were riding their bicycles and had taken Tasoula and me for a ride. We both felt very important sitting on these huge bikes.

A crowd of village children watched as a rough football field was prepared, with two poles placed at either end for the goals.

The teams kicked the ball and were moving it between their legs and sometimes hitting it with their heads. Each time Heraklis had the ball I cheered him on as he kicked the ball down the field. I yelled with excitement, "Come on, Heraklis. Come on, Heraklis!" I loved seeing him play.

It was a very exciting and friendly game. It was a game for all to remember.

Heraklis' friends climbed back on their bikes and Tasoula and I had our photos taken sitting on the bikes. We were really pleased to sit on the huge bikes and then we waved to them as they rode their bikes back to Florina. Then we headed home as well.

Heraklis held Tasoula's and my hands as we ran inside the house. And he yelled out, "We had a great game of football down by the river and our team won. It was a wonderful game and I kicked the first goal". He was very excited as we were all going to have our last meal together before he caught the bus.

But *Baba* was fuming as he yelled, "The clouds are building and it looks like rain. We could have done with your help and what did you do? You went off kicking a ball. Where's your sense of responsibility? What have you gained from that?"

Baba was angry, annoyed and hurt. His eldest son was leaving. What would he face in another land? Could he handle the language barriers? How will he cope? *Baba* did not know how to express his sorrow.

As soon as my brother stopped talking, my *Baba* started yelling at him

"You silly, lazy, good for nothing fool. You forgot your responsibilities! While your *Mama* and I worked you were off enjoying yourself. I'll kill you!" And then my *Baba* grabbed his shotgun. "You had your party to say goodbye to all. But no, you had to have a game of football too. I'll teach you a lesson to abandon your work!"

"Gianni! Stop it. What in the name of Heaven has got into you? Heraklis is leaving in few hours. He just wanted to say goodbye to his mates," *Mama* cried out in his defence.

My brother raced outside to miss *Baba's* swipe. *Baba* was in pursuit, yelling and screaming abuse at him. My *Baba* was a very quiet person, but if someone or something upset him, well you then had to watch out, as his temper would really be like a hurricane and you really had to get out of his way.

I had never seen *Baba* so angry and yelling like he did that day. He chased my brother all through the village. We did not know what was wrong with him.

Mama had cooked my brother's favorite meal, bean soup. This was for all of us to have a last meal as a family. And his *Baba* was yelling and screaming and acting like a madman. *'Ta babala tou ehi?'* (Had *Baba* gone mad?) This was *Mama's* favourite saying if *Baba* was angry.

The hours flew by and there was no sign of them. The bus was leaving at 7.00 p.m. *Mama* packed my brother's few belongings lovingly into a little suitcase. There was one shirt and two boxer shorts, one pair of pajamas that she had made for him, one jumper, two pairs of socks and two singlets. She also wrapped in a white tea towel, two boiled eggs, crusty bread, feta cheese and some olives. She then wrapped it all in white paper a few times, hoping to keep the food fresh. On the bed beside this little suitcase were my brother's shoes, socks, shirt, tie and his suit. When Heraklis had picked up the suit from the tailor he wore it and Eleftherios and Heraklis had their photo taken in Florina. We thought they looked so handsome. *Mama* was crying and wringing her hands as she prayed and kept looking through the window, as she kept on muttering, "What is wrong with the man, has he lost his mind?" I kept on looking at *Mama* wanting to help, but all I could do was just watch her wring her hands and lovingly pack her son's things.

Suddenly my brother Heraklis burst in.

"Heraklis! Where is your *Baba*?" *Mama* asked.

"I don't know and I don't care," he said.

"How can you say that?" *Mama* demanded.

"He is the one wanting to kill me. I must get dressed as the bus leaves in 30 minutes" Heraklis said.

"Your clothes are ready." A dark suit was on his bed. *Mama* had scraped and saved to send her firstborn away looking like a man. His small suitcase was sitting beside the clothes he was to wear. He was well off compared to others.

My brother got dressed as *Mama* shed tears. Then we all walked to the bus, *Mama*, Eleftherios, Tasoula and I. The entire village was there. The bus was filling up; there were men, women and children leaving the village. There was laughter, tears, happiness and sadness. Heraklis hugged each one of us and then quickly hopped on to the bus.

My *Mama's* tears rolled down her cheeks as she wrung her hands. Tasoula was clinging on to my Mama's legs while I held Eleftherios' hand. We watched with fascination. *Mama* had one consolation in that *Baba's* cousin, Thanaso, with his wife Taso, and their children, Stavroula and Soufoula and Christos, were also migrating at the same time.

We all waved at the bus as it started down the road.

Whose turn was it next? People waited for their migration papers, visas and passports.

Baba came walking up the road dragging his feet and his shotgun. He looked tired and worn out.

Mama yelled at him, "Gianni, have you gone mad? Your son has gone and you didn't even say goodbye to him. Instead you chased him over the fields, valleys and hills for hours."

"Yes I did. He will remember that. That was my farewell party for him; he must never forget his responsibilities. If he does, his *Baba* will be after him with the shotgun."

"Responsibilities? What responsibilities? Threatening him with a shotgun? Give me that stupid thing. I have half a mind to shoot you! Do you hear me! You look so tired; you can hardly stand on your feet!" *Mama* yelled.

"Olga, I'm hungry," *Baba* said quietly.

"You're hungry? You are always hungry," *Mama* yelled.

Mama looked at the shotgun. She hated guns. So many innocent people died. How dare Gianni chase his son with the gun? She checked the shotgun, breaking it open and looking at the barrels. Then she said, surprised, "It is empty! It is not loaded?" she exclaimed.

"Of course it's empty, woman. Do you think I am stupid? I love my son. I just wanted to teach him a lesson."

"A lesson? It is the weirdest thing I have ever seen. Is that the way to say goodbye to your son, Gianni? When will you see him again?" my *Mama* yelled.

"Soon!" And *Baba* grinned and winked at us. He had already thought of joining his son in the new country. Hoping that in that land they would find peace and hope and a better future.

That night when everyone had gone to bed I was really concerned about my parents so I sneaked out and watched them in the living room. *Baba* held *Mama* close as he said to her, "Do not worry, my love, we will follow our son soon," and he kissed her gently.

I giggled as I watched them; it was so good to see them happy.

Mama said quietly to *Baba* as she had her back to me, "Who is that?"

"Olympia," he said and he winked at me. I went off to bed feeling happy.

#31
Migrating to Australia

After my brother Heraklis, my *Thea* Taso and *Theo* Thanaso left in April 1954 and other people from the village followed them. *Theo* Christopher and *Thea* Ourania and all their children, Anna, Athanassis and Arhodoula, *Theo* Stellios and *Thea* Chrissy with their son, George, and their daughter, Anastasia, migrated in August that year. There were others who applied to migrate. The village was slowly emptying. These people migrated to Australia under the Inter Government European Contract of Migration in 1954.

Heraklis travelled on the boat *Cyrenia*. He arrived in Melbourne on the 21st of May, 1954, was greeted in Port Melbourne and taken to Bonegilla Migrant Reception Centre by train where there were 540 other immigrants. Bonegilla is a small Victorian town 15 Km east of Albury/ Wodonga, on the border of Victoria and New South Wales. It was the former Army training facility, but from 1947 Bonegilla was used as a Migrant Reception Centre and was the temporary home for more than 320000 migrants between 1947 and 1971. It was their first home in Australia and they were given a bed and food while the Government also assisted them to find work. They all came to improve their lives and for better opportunities. My *Thea* Taso and *Theo* Thanaso found work in an iron foundry in Wollongong, NSW. Others went to the Hydro Electricity Scheme in the Snowy Mountains, or to various factories or sugar-cane farms in Northern Queensland.

My brother Heraklis and the friends he had met on the boat, Theodoros, his wife, Ebdoxia, and their son, Stellios, were offered work at the railway depot in Port Melbourne. They all rented bedrooms with friends and worked long hours with overtime in order to save enough money for a deposit on a home. Heraklis only really rented a bed as he shared the bedroom in a house with other migrants. This old house was in Fitzroy and often he would visit relatives, particularly on a Friday, to have a home-cooked meal, especially *Thea* Chrissy and *Theo* Stellios or *Thea* Taso and *Theo* Thanaso. They would cook bean or the lentil soup that he loved as we did not eat meat on Fridays.

As soon as he saved enough deposit, Heraklis bought a house in Northcote, an outer suburb of Melbourne. A year later he sponsored us through the Inter Churches Migration Scheme, which meant we had to pay to come to Australia. This was approximately £300 for all the family.

We then had to wait to see if we had been accepted. When we received our letter of acceptance we then had to go through medical examinations and fill in all the appropriate papers. We also had to obtain our passports and immigration papers. All we needed now was money to relocate the family.

We all continued working in the fields, but that was not enough for the extra money that was needed. *Baba* and Eleftherios started working every weekend in the lime pits. I remember this quite clearly as I had to take their lunch to them. It was a long walk to the pits because they were on the outskirts of the village. When I came to the place where *Mama* told me I would find them I could not believe there were so many men and young boys working there. They all had large hammers, which they were using to break huge, white boulders. It was then put into wheelbarrows and then taken to a huge pit where there was smokelike clouds rising into the air as the lime was bubbling away. All the men were covered with white dust.

They paid *Baba* wages, but they did not pay Eleftherios as they said he was only helping his father and they only paid for the man, not the boys, even though Eleftherios could lift a hammer and work just as hard as the men. *Baba* and Eleftherios argued the point, but the pit owners were aware that we were leaving for overseas and they simply said to them, "You can sue us if you like," knowing that *Baba* and Eleftherios did not have the money or the time to do that.

With all this extra work and frustration *Mama* kept getting colds and coughs and in the end she was very sick. She had acute tonsillitis, but the doctors in Florina would not operate on her and she had to go to Thessaloniki. She had to recover first before they would operate and take her tonsils out. *Baba* and Tasoula had gone with her and they all stayed with my *Thea* Sapfo and *Theo* George.

Eleftherios and I had to remain behind to harvest the wheat. My brother was only 16 years old and I was seven. We both worked at cutting the wheat then tying it into bundles, putting it in the cart and then taking it to the commune where wheat was being thrashed by a mule turning a large stone by going around and around. It was very hard work as I helped my brother. For lunch we had boiled potatoes, tomatoes, spring onions, olives and feta cheese.

One day Eleftherios said, "Olympia, could you please make the potatoes with eggs?" The potatoes were already boiled as Eleftherios would light the wood stove very early in the morning and boil a big batch, which was enough for both of us.

"*Andaxi tha do magirespo* (all right I will cook that for us), Eleftherios." I put the big frying pan on the wood stove and added the oil. I chopped the boiled potatoes and dropped them into the frying pan. I stirred the potatoes until they were well browned, broke a few eggs and put them in with the potatoes and stirred this until the eggs were all scrambled. I put this in a container and took it to the field where Eleftherios was working,, for our lunch.

When I got there I spread out a small tablecloth with two tin plates and forks, and then served all the mashed food on the plates. We had cold water to drink. I had filled the clay pot from the spring that flowed in the gully. I did exactly as *Mama* used to do, so that we could have lunch under the big old tree. When I had all of this ready I then called out, "Eleftherios, lunch is ready".

We both sat under the tree and I watched him eat. He then said, "Olympia, this is the best food I have ever tasted".

I was so proud of myself; I then gulped down the mashed food too. And guess what, poor Eleftherios got that food every day until our parents came back!

He worked so hard that summer. It was incredible that a 16-year-old could handle all that work. Sometimes I look back and wonder if I was not more of a hindrance than a help. We both had lots of laughs while yelling and screaming at each other. I would try to tie the wheat bundles, and when I couldn't I would play and throw wheat at him or roll on it. He would get annoyed as I would not concentrate. So he would tie the wheat in bundles and yell at me, *"Skatoula"* (You little shit). It took a few attempts before we could tie it in bundles. And I did not help by playing up so much. But we did have lots of laughs together.

When our parents came back, *Mama's* health was not the best, and often she would be in bed so I had to cook. She would tell me what to do and I would try to cook for all the family.

Baba started selling the animals and that was a very sad time for all of us as they were precious to us and they were my friends. I often would talk to the animals, especially when *Baba* had to feed them and clean them. I loved talking to my friend the grey donkey. He was so special and he would always greet me with a nudge. He knew that I had a carrot or apple or whatever I could find in the kitchen for him. Whenever I went in the shed he was the first to greet me. I loved spending time with him, especially to brush and pat and care for him. I was so unhappy that we had to sell all the animals, but especially my little grey donkey that I had seen being born; he was my friend, my mate.

A big old gypsy who had gold earrings on his earlobes and a red scarf around his neck came around to look at 'my' donkey. *Mama* often told us to be wary of gypsies as they would take children. So when he came and started looking in the mouth of my favorite animal I was upset and so annoyed that I started yelling at him "Don't touch him! He is my friend! I saw him being born! He comes to me when I call him. You can't have him! Do you hear?" And I started hitting the gypsy while still yelling at him. I did not want him to take my friends away. Tears were flowing down my face.

"Woo, she is a fiery one. I could do with one of them. Is she for sale too?" the gypsy asked.

Baba grabbed me and held my hand and cried, "No, she is not!"

Then he looked at me and said firmly, "Olympia, we have to go to Australia. We cannot take our animals with us. I do not like selling the animals, but we have no choice. We have to sell them."

The gypsy opened the donkey's mouth and looked carefully at all her teeth, went around prodding and checking her then lifted each of her hooves to examine them. After he had done that he did the same to the colt. In the end the gypsy bought the colt and the donkey. I was hurt. I did not want him to take them; I just did not like that man. I sat on the steps crying, *Baba* came and picked me up in his arms and took me to *Mama* and said, "Olga, do something with your daughter, she will not stop crying."

Mama then yelled at me, "Olympia, stop that! You are not a baby; you are a young lady now. (I was fully-grown up! I was seven years old, after all, and I should have known better.) We have no choice. We have to sell all the animals, or leave them with your *Giagia*. And she certainly cannot look after all these animals, and besides we do need the money for our trip to Australia."

Mama was the real practical one, not one to show caring, even if my feelings were hurt.

Slowly our animals were sold one by one, the pigs, the goats, the ox, and the cow, or we gave them away. Finally the only ones left were our dogs, Lisa and her pups, and the chickens, which were to go to our neighbours before we left.

We had been waiting for our immigration papers to come and it was taking weeks; my parents were getting frustrated. Then one day one of our roosters started jumping up on the windowsill and pecking on the window-pane.

"Olympia, will you stop putting that rooster on the windowsill? It will wreck the flowers in the window boxes. My beautiful red geraniums are growing so well, they are my pride and joy. The rooster will dirty the window pane, take it away, " *Mama* yelled at me.

"*Mama*,I am not putting that rooster on the windowsill, it is doing it by itself."

"Well, will you just go and take it away," she called.

I took the little red rooster and gave it a hug and a kiss, went and placed it with the other hens and then trotted off to *Giagia* Malamati's and asked her, "Would you like some help, *Giagia*?"

"Olympia, I would love you to collect the duck eggs. They lay them everywhere, even in the pond," she replied, and handed me her little basket for the eggs and sat in her favorite spot outside the door as she watched me collect the eggs. What a wonderful excuse it was for me to paddle in the pond! I felt that if I was away from *Mama* I would not get into trouble again. Little did I know! I had a wonderful time playing with the ducks and frolicking in the pond. I then gave Sarko, *Giagia's* dog, a big hug and a kiss and *Giagia* laughed at me and said, "You funny little girl, you always give the animals a hug and a kiss, what about a hug and kiss for your *Giagia*". So I gave her a big hug and kiss, then trotted back home. When I did go home, my clothes and sandals were all soaked. Oooh! *Mama* was not very impressed with me again as she said, "I just do not understand how you manage to get so dirty all the time. Go and get changed and wash before dinner. Go on, get going".

That evening *Mama* said to us, "That little red rooster kept pecking on the window pane today, Gianni. I thought at first Olympia was playing games with me. But she was not around when the rooster kept pecking at the window pane again and again. I believe we will have a message because of the pecking. I am sure we will hear something." She then crossed herself saying a little prayer "*Tou Christou I dunami na ine mazimas*," (Christ's strength be with us) and hoped that the message would be good.

Sure enough, the next day we did receive a wonderful letter. We were all at *Giagia* Malamati's place helping her clean her barn to store the hay and the produce we had. We did not hear the postman shouting at us; we were all laughing and talking as we cleaned the barn. Suddenly we heard a scream. We all raced outside to see Sarko, the St Bernard, with the postman's bottom in his mouth. It looked so funny, but the postman was not impressed. *Baba* said he was lucky Sarko did not bite him as he held him in his jaws. He was eager to deliver our registered mail and he knew we were at Malamati's place as he could hear us there. Usually the dog barked as he was always tied under the quince tree. But this time the postman was anxious to deliver the mail to us, because he was aware we were waiting for our immigration papers.

Mama had waited for the postman every day and asked him if there was mail for us. *Mama* said later, probably the postman wanted to get a tip. But in his enthusiasm he had forgotten the dog and had just raced in to deliver the letter and had not thought that the dog could break his chain. *Baba* grabbed the dog by his collar and got it off the postman's bottom. The postman handed *Baba* this thick envelope and did not wait for his tip, which usually was a bottle of wine, a dozen eggs, or, if he was lucky enough, a chicken.

Our papers had come! We were leaving for Australia! We were all thrilled and happy that we would be joining Heraklis in Australia. But first we had to go through our medical test so we all travelled to Thessaloniki for that. It was a great family gathering as we met our cousins, Spiro and Kosta, and *Thea* Sapfo and *Theo* George once again. *Mama* warned me, "When you go to see the doctors laugh so he does not see your huge appendix scar".

When it was my turn to see the doctor, he put his stethoscope on my chest to examine me. I started giggling each time and he also laughed and the nurse laughed too and we all had a great laughing session. At the end of the examination he gave me a lollipop. I was really pleased. The passports and immigration papers were to be posted to us. We all passed the medical examination and we were told that they would notify us when we would be leaving and what boat we would be boarding at the port of Piraeus.

Mama had lots of sorting and packing to do, figuring out what to take and what to leave behind. I had a few toys that were given to me by *Theas* or cousins. They were hand-me-downs except for my bus, my real treasure which I got when I was in hospital. There were a couple of rag dolls that various *Theas* had given me over the years and my abacus on which I had learnt to count. I called my friends together and we sat down and I handed out the few toys I had. *Mama* said, "Olympia, what have you done?" as she watched the little neighbouring children with a toy each, especially the bus that *Mama* had bought for me.

"I gave everyone a toy, *Mama*," I said, proudly.

"I know you did, but why did you do that, Olympia?" *Mama* queried.

"It's all right *Mama*. When we get to Australia there will be lots and lots of toys there," I said.

"Yes, but you have to work, earn some money, and save up in order to buy toys. They do not grow on trees you know. Olympia, you are impossible."

Somehow *Mama* and I did not see eye-to-eye. *Baba* had a grin on his face. Whenever I saw that grin I just always felt better.

We received our letter saying we would be boarding the boat the *Skaugum* in Piraeus in July.

My parents and Tasoula went to Kastoria to say their goodbyes to *Thea* Anna and *Theo* George. Eleftherios and I stayed behind and continued to work. We would pick the various vegetables and then we would sell them on the side of the road to people who went past our front yard. This year there was no pickling and drying of fruit. We had to sell everything fresh. All our vegetables and fruit, including our delicious tomatoes, had to be picked and sold daily.

I would start early in the morning on the side of the road selling the various vegetables and fruit such as tomatoes, cucumbers, rockmelons and watermelons, plums and apricots. While Eleftherios was picking them I was selling them to people who went past our front yard. As we were on the main road it was easy. We had set up a little stall and sold all that we could pick.

"Fresh cucumbers just picked today, they are crisp and juicy," I would yell when I saw people coming. There were people from seven other villages who had to go past our village on their way to Florina, and so there were always people walking or riding on their carts past our place. It was great as most people looked at me being so young and would take pity and buy something.

When my parents and Tasoula returned from seeing my *Thea* Anna and *Theo* George, *Mama* had to pack all the things that we would take with us. It was not easy for her trying to fit all the family clothes and all our belongings into a trunk. My *Thea* had given *Mama* an old suitcase that we used for our everyday clothes for the boat trip, while the trunk held all of our possessions for our new home.

Mama had made some of our clothes and packed them into the big trunk. To choose what to take and what to leave was very hard and she often shed tears as she packed and unpacked the trunk. She would put things in and then she would take them out. In the end she chose to pack her weaving gear, her religious icons, a blue platter and the pink silk divan cover that belonged to her mother. It was her mother's wedding present to her. Blankets, rugs and our heavy winter clothes were also put in the trunk.

Mama then prepared a big basket with cucumbers, tomatoes, cheese, olives, boiled eggs, spring onions, pickles, jam and bread for our journey. She had everything ready for the next day when we all got dressed in our best gear and then had photos taken in the front yard of our house with *Giagia* Malamati, as she was staying behind.

Early the next day, with the other families who were migrating, we caught the bus in the front of the *Cafenio* in Tropaioukhos, for Florina. I can still remember all the different smells of the food that people had brought along. There were salamis, garlic, sausages, jams, pickles, cheeses, vegetables, fruit, walnuts, peanuts and whatever they could carry. All this food was taken to keep the families fed for the trip and was carried in bags or baskets.

We boarded the bus with our friends, the Emmanouilidis family. We were migrating together with the parents, Thanassis and Katina, and their daughter, Giannoula, who was 16 (the same age as Eleftherios), and their young son Stratos, who was three and a half years old. We were travelling together as their son had also sponsored them to Australia. Their son, Theofanis Emmanouilidis, left Tropaioukhos on the 16th of January, 1954 (three months earlier than Heraklis). He had made his own little suitcase and had arrived in Port Melbourne Australia on the 17th of February 1954.

The bus took us to Florina where we were met by all the relatives. There my *Thea* Giannoula and all her children hugged and kissed us and we all said our goodbyes. Another bus took us from Florina to Thessaloniki, a journey that took us two hours 45 minutes. We stayed there with my *Thea* Sapfo for a couple of days. *Thea* loved to have her hair permed and colored so for the first time my mother had her hair cut, colored and permed. That was, of course, after much encouragement from my *Thea*.

Thessaloniki is named after the sister of Alexander the Great; it is Greece's second-largest city and has some of the greatest archeological treasures. In the couple of days we were there, we did the tourist thing and visited the church of Saint Dimitrios, which is one of the oldest churches, first built in 313AD, and is the largest in Greece with Byzantine mosaics adorning the inside.

Mama, with lots of other young children was baptised there when they arrived as refugees from Thrace in 1922. We visited the cathedral of Haghia Sophia, which was an eighth century church, and the White Tower on the waterfront, which is the symbol of the city. It was used by the sultans when the Ottomans ruled, as a prison and a place of execution.

We caught the bus to Athens, which took us about nine hours to get there. Of course I kept on asking, “Are we there yet?” In the end I fell asleep and when we arrived in Athens we stayed at a very old hostel that was musty and damp and smelled, but we could not afford a better hotel. However, we were all very tired and we slept well.

The next day we visited many historical places in Athens, the Acropolis, and some old churches and saw the *evzonas* (the changing of the guards).

We then caught the bus to the port city of Piraeus and very late in the afternoon we boarded the *Skaugum*, a Norwegian cargo boat. It was late and I remember I was very tired. They put all women and children on one side of the boat where there were lots of bunks, one on top of another, while the men were on the other side of the boat.

The *M V Skaugum* was originally launched in Germany in 1940, but because of the war it was not completed. It was used as a cargo boat and then rebuilt as an immigrant ship in 1948. The ship was 11,626 gross tons, had a speed of 15 knots and accommodated 1700 passengers. It was finally scrapped in 1972.

We all waved goodbye to people below and there were many tears with people wondering whether they would see their loved ones again.

#32

THE BOAT TRIP!

Everyone was excited, but also sad, leaving behind families and friends and their homeland, the place that we called home. We all wondered if we could cope with the long boat trip and whether we would be strong enough to face the hardships that we may have in the new country, Australia, a country about which we knew very little.

Late at night the siren sounded and the *Skaugum* began to move. Slowly everything that was familiar began to disappear from our eyes until we were surrounded by the vastness of the sea.

As the boat had originally departed from Venice, there were many other migrants from elsewhere in Europe. Everyone was looking to better themselves, to improve their lives, after living through the horror of the World War II and the civil war in Greece. They were all heading to their 'New Land', no wars, no persecutions and no hunger, but hoping for peace and prosperity in their new country. *Mama*, Tasoula and me, with many other women and children, all had to share toilets and showers. We would line up for our turn we laughed and joked and we communicated with lots of signs as we all spoke different languages.

The boat had been a cargo boat, but now it carried the human cargo to a new land. It also had a very strong smell about it and that really upset many people. *Mama* would often hold a lemon to her nose to overcome the strong smell of the boat and to keep her from being sick.

When we arrived to our first port, which was Port Said, there were many people selling their various products. From carpets, clothes, shoes and slippers, scarves and fruits that we had never seen. It was the very first time that I had seen bananas. They were selling them and people bought to taste them. My parents bought some bananas and we all enjoyed this strange fruit, which was sweet and squishy.

Mama also bought a beautiful small carpet and she was bargaining with the trader when he jumped aboard. We were all together, but he approached Tasoula. My sister was a beautiful child, always clean and tidy and she had delightful blue eyes and lovely fair curls. He was a black Arab and he went to touch her curly hair, but my sister screamed and the man jumped over the rails very quickly. But he upset her and it took my *Mama* ages to calm her down.

The next port we headed for was Bombay, and we sailed slowly through the channel to the port of Bombay. It was a lovely place with tropical palms in the distance and with people selling lots of items and many kinds of fruit. My parents bought fresh bananas again, which we thoroughly enjoyed, but it was very noisy in the port as all the traders were trying to outbid each other to sell their various items.

Again the siren sounded and we headed for the great ocean. Our next stop was Fremantle and that was when the Indian Ocean really got rough. *Mama* and Tasoula ended up in the sick bay. I had to go with *Baba* and Eleftherios to sleep in the men's dormitory. I loved it as they all spoilt me and gave me peanuts and whatever lollies they had.

Baba, Eleftherios and I would go for breakfast, lunch and dinner and we would be the only ones turning up, as the seas were really rough. The steward serving us could not believe us as he often crossed himself and spoke in his language. He chuckled at us, as the three of us would not miss our meals, even though the seas were rough, but that did not worry us, especially if they had lentil soup, my favorite dish, on the menu.

I loved the boat trip and often I would just wander around and would look from the front of the boat and watch the dolphins jump through the waves. I was so fascinated and thrilled to watch those wonderful animals.

On the 10th of August, 1955 our boat *MV Skaugum,* bound for Australia, crossed the equator from the Northern to the Southern Hemisphere with great celebrations, and each one of us was issued a certificate of 'IMPERIUM NEPTUNI REGIS' as we were initiated into the S**olemn Mysteries** of **the Ancient Order of the Deep.**

The seas were very rough and we were worried, as *Mama* was so sick we did not think she could survive the trip.

We arrived in Fremantle and we hoped that the seas would not be too rough from then on. But that was not the case. As we crossed the Great Australian Bight the seas became progressively worse and *Mama* was permanently in the sick bay.

On the 23rd of August, 1955 we arrived in Port Melbourne. There was a big crowd to greet all of us. The 620 assisted migrants were taken to the train to go to Bonegilla and then slowly the rest of us were allowed to disembark. It was very exciting and *Mama* felt better as the boat was now in port and it was not rough any more. She came down from the sick bay and helped pack all of our belongings in the suitcase. She said to me, "Olympia, would you look after your sister and the suitcase while I go and see if we can see Heraklis in the crowd below, as there are so many people". When *Mama* left I said to my sister, "Tasoula, now just sit on the suitcase so no-one will take it and I will go and see if I can find Heraklis".

So off I went, but there were people rushing here and there. They were all very excited and nearly trampled on me. I then thought the best way was to go and look through the porthole and see if I could see Heraklis and Australia. I went to the toilets and then climbed on to a toilet seat and tried to push the porthole open. While I was doing that I hit my head as the porthole opened. I found myself stuck in the hole and all I could see was lots of water below me. My body hung out of the porthole and my legs were dangling inside, but I was stuck and blood was flowing down my face as I had caught my eyebrow on the porthole catch. I started yelling for help, but everyone was on the other side of the boat. There was no-one around and I could feel myself slipping, heading for the water. All I could think of was that there I was again and that I would get into trouble once more. I hung on tightly so that I would not to fall in to the water.

I screamed for help hoping that someone would hear me and pull me out of this porthole. Suddenly the steward who used to cross himself pulled me in and started crossing himself again. He yelled at me in his language and raced me to the sick bay. The doctor looked at me then cleaned my face and stitched the wound on my eyebrow. They were talking to me, but I could not understand what they were saying.

Then a young lady come up and spoke Greek to me and asked who my parents were so she could contact them. She then used the public address system to page my parents. *Mama* came up and she saw my face all bandaged and she could not believe how I managed to get into trouble again in such a short space of time. She thanked God and crossed herself, like the steward, then grabbed my hand and pulled me along and said, "We have seen Heraklis and he is waiting for us to disembark".

We disembarked and made our way through Customs. It was lovely to see all the family together and Heraklis exclaimed, when he saw the bandages, "What have you been up to again, Olympia?"

"Heraklis, I tried to find you, but I got caught in the porthole," I told him and they all laughed and shook their heads.

Mama finished off by saying "Certainly St George was looking after her again, as the steward rescued her from falling overboard".

We all got into a taxi. In those days there were no seatbelts in cars and we sat on *Mama's* and *Baba's* laps. All our belongings, the suitcase, the basket that originally contained all our food (which was all eaten earlier in the trip) and the carpet *Mama* had bought in Port Said, somehow fitted into the taxi, while our trunk was to be delivered direct to our new home.

Heraklis had bought a house in Northcote, an outer suburb of Mebourne in Victoria. It was a white timber home with two large bay windows at the front, three bedrooms, bathroom, kitchen, living room and laundry and we all loved it. It had a huge block and *Baba* decided that he would plant his olive tree, grapevine, lemon tree, fruit trees and have a big vegetable garden there.

#33
We move to Richmond

While we all loved the house in Northcote, we were there for only a few weeks, as the house, unknown to us, had been sold before we arrived in Australia. It was a luxury home compared with what we had in the village. It even had rose-coloured carpets with huge flowers on it and an outside toilet! It was close to a little shopping centre for necessities. We found buying bread every day was a luxury for us and the bread we ate when we first arrived was incredible as it was so fresh! Every day I would walk to the milk bar to buy six loaves of bread and the shopkeeper could not believe how much bread we ate. He often said to me, "You must have a big family". But I just smiled and bought the bread as I could not understand what he said. When my brother Heraklis (who was now known as Hercules) would buy the bread he told the shopkeeper that there were only six people in the family. But he still shook his head each time I bought the bread.

Friends advised Hercules that the house would be too far from the city for all of us, so he put the house on the market to sell before we arrived in Australia. It sold very quickly. He looked for a house that was very central and then bought a house in Richmond.

Once the house at Richmond was settled, Hercules asked *Mama*, Tasoula and me to go and clean the house so that on the following weekend we could all move in. All the men were at work during the week and could not help with the cleaning. *Mama*, my sister and I did not speak a word of English. We had to find our new home in Richmond only with a note that my brother wrote. We took a bucket, rags, mop and broom with us on the tram from Northcote to the City. From the City we then had to find another tram that went along Swan St, and that took us to Church St, Richmond. But we had to go past Flinders St Railway station, with which we were all fascinated as it was such a huge station and there were lots of people coming and going.

Hercules had written down which tram to take and how many stops it was before we had to take another tram to get to 399 Church St, Richmond. He had given us two pieces of paper to show to the tram conductor each time we got on a tram so that we could buy a ticket. Mama would put out her hand with some money in order to buy our ticket. She showed them a handful of money as she did not know the currency. It was all new to her.

We had to count the tram stops before we got off the first tram. From there we caught the second tram and again showed the conductor the instructions on the paper and the handful of money to buy our tickets. We counted off the tram stops and then got off that tram at the corner of Swan St and Church St Richmond. From there, following my brother's instructions, we went up the hill, as he had told us, in order to find our new home. We had to find 399 Church St, Richmond and we walked from the tram up the hill and started looking for the house, all the time carrying our cleaning gear.

We came to a beautiful two-storey home surrounded by lovely gardens and with a black iron-rail fence around it. We all admired that house. It looked so grand and we hoped that it was ours. It had a square golden sign painted at the front gate and people were going in and out of the house. We found out that it was a doctor's surgery. Dr Grogan. What a disappointment!

Our new home was across the road from the doctor's surgery. On one side of number 399 was a milk bar which was owned by two ladies. It was so handy as we could buy our milk, bread, ice-cream and lollies there. That shop was later sold to Jack Dyer, the famous Richmond footballer; all his family worked in that milk bar.

On the other side of our house was another terraced home, owned by Mrs. Weatherley, an old lady who had two little dogs, Trixie and Patch, which were Jack Russells. I would often visit her to play with her dogs and she would let me run up and down her stairs as her little dogs chased me, which exercised her dogs and kept me amused.

There were all terraced two-storey brick homes around our house. They looked really big to us. The front gate to number 399 screeched when we pushed it open. There was a tiled veranda at the front of the house and a small green hedge at the fence. *Mama* put the huge key in the door and tried to unlock the door. It was a very heavy door. She pushed it, but then she had to really shove it before she could open the door. It was a two storey house but it looked as though it had not been lived in for a long time.

Through the front door was a long passage. On the left of the passage was the first room and there was a second room near the staircase. As we walked through we saw that the huge front room on the left had a big, open fireplace in it, and a large window that looked out on to the front veranda. Originally it was probably a living room. The room next to this was a smaller one, but again it had an open fireplace and a window looking out to a covered patio. There was one step down to the kitchen and dining room. This was a very small room that had a small stainless sink, a gas stove in the chimney corner and a meter where we had to put threepence in each time to make the gas stove work. And often when *Mama* was cooking the money would run out, so Tasoula and I had to race next-door to the shop to get change of threepence to put in the meter so that the stove would be working again. In the bedrooms there were very old carpets and the floors in the rest of the house were covered with a very dirty green lino. The entire place was filthy and looked as though it had never seen a broom or mop.

We then climbed the stairs to a small landing. On the right we came to another bedroom. The views from the window were over the houses at the rear – there were lots of older houses at the back of our home. Then up six steps to the first floor was another bedroom on the right and from the window in this room you could see a tall white building in the distance, which was in the Botanical Gardens. On the top landing was a huge bedroom on this floor, which could have been a lounge, or another living room. It also had a huge open fireplace and two large windows that looked out on to a veranda and to Church St along which the trams travelled.

All the rooms were full of dust, cobwebs and rubbish and the place needed a very good clean-up. *Mama* decided to tackle one room at a time. So we started with the upstairs large room first. We cleaned the fireplace and then swept the floors and *Mama* would fill the bucket with rubbish. Tasoula and I would take it downstairs into the little back yard. *Mama* then cleaned the huge windows, as they were really dirty.

In the very small back yard was a tiny herb garden in one corner and there was a clothesline with a stick to hold up the middle of the line. The laundry consisted of cement double tubs and a boiler to wash the clothes; there was also a huge old bathtub there, and the floor was rough concrete. The bathroom and laundry were together at the back and the toilet was separate, right at the rear of the yard.

We worked hard helping *Mama* clean the house and at the end of the day the house looked better, but there was still much to be done to make it livable. We then headed for home. We had to remember the way and show the conductor again our little piece of paper to show him where we were heading.

Hercules had a friend who had an old truck and the following day we packed what little furniture we had on to that truck. There were the beds he had bought at the second-hand place for all of us, and our belongings, loaded on this old truck. That included our few possessions from Greece, and our trunk. We all piled into the back of the truck and moved to the new house.

Hercules, Eleftherios (who was now known as Eric) and *Baba* pulled up the old carpets and then painted each room and laid down new lino. All of our work certainly freshened up the place. *Mama* soon found out where the second-hand shops were so she bought some cupboards for each room. In the kitchen she put a cupboard that had sliding, stained-glass windows at the top and small doors below. We did not have a lot of furniture, but we had more than we had in Greece.

Baba worked at GMH and used the trams to travel to Port Melbourne. Hercules worked in the railway depot in Port Melbourne. Eric worked with my *Thea* Taso at Nielsons, an electrical factory. None of us spoke any English except my brother Hercules, who had learnt English at high school. He also went to night school to improve his English.

When Tasoula and I started school we could not speak English. Our first day at school was very daunting, as we could not understand a word of the English language that our teacher spoke. There was a Cypriot Greek girl named Sylvia in our class and she interpreted for us. She had lovely, curly black hair and a very beautiful, round face. Tasoula was put into grade one and I went into grade two. The class all had desks with little inkwells on them. We would use ink pens to write with and there were ink monitors every morning to refill them, which I found fascinating. I also liked raising the desk top, but the teacher would stare at me because it screeched each time. The teacher was not impressed as often students would lift the desks tops, most times on purpose, and there would be the screeching noise, and he would yell at us.

At the school there were two Cypriot girls, both named Androulas, and Sylvia. Lubinka and her brother Peter were from Yugoslavia. We were the only migrant children at the school. With Lubinka and the two Androulas we built up a friendship. We seemed to stick together, as we were able to communicate with each other. We loved playing sport more than schoolwork and often I would stay after school to play with my new friends. When *Baba* or *Mama* came to pick us up I would say, "I will just play one more game and then I'll come", whether it was rounders, or basketball (or any other kind of sport!).

I loved playing with a ball, but we did not have a big enough yard to play, but at the back of our house there was a lane. Off this lane there was our neighbour, who had a lovely brick wall, which was great for me to bounce my ball. I loved bouncing my ball on her wall for hours; she did not mind me doing that as she was deaf. However, she had three porcelain flying ducks hanging on her wall, and if I hit the ball too hard the odd time, they would fall and break. She would come and yell at me for breaking her ducks and poor *Mama* had to go and buy new ducks for her. I had done that a few times and at the end *Mama* banned me from bouncing my ball there.

Living at Richmond with hardly any back yard we missed the freedom and freshness of the country. Tasoula was missing the animals and her friends from Tropaioukhos and the language barrier was traumatic for her (but these days, as my husband points out, she speaks more like an Australian than I do!). She would get sick and cried often, as she wanted to go back to Greece and to our animals. I loved it in Australia as I did not have to work. I enjoyed going to the matinee pictures every Saturday at our local Globe cinema. It was down the street, across the road from the Italian coffee shop from where they sold lovely gelati ice-cream, which I loved, but it was expensive and often we could not afford it. It was a treat for us now and then. The queues at the cinema were long and noisey as all the children were excited to see the matinee. I could only go if only my sister or Lubinka, my friend, came with me. I would beg every week to go, especially if there were cowboys and Indians. *Mama* would then give us one shilling each and that would be for our ticket and for our ice-cream or lollies. Tasoula did not like going, but I would drag her along as I was not allowed to go by myself, so she had to come with me. When there was a cowboys and Indians film, and there was any fighting, she would hide under the seat, or put her hands on her face, and would say "Have they finished shooting yet?" I would then tell her when it was safe for her to watch the picture.

Lubinka sometimes would come with us to the Greek Church on Sundays or I would go with her to her Sunday school. One Sunday her Sunday school was having a picnic so I went with her. It was great fun as we all hopped on a bus, which took us to a large park. We had lots of games, a race with an egg on a spoon, sack races, ball games and lots of food. I won the sack race and the egg and spoon race and I was given a beautiful book, which thrilled me. We then had a large table with a lovely white tablecloth and lots and lots of food. There was fruit, cakes, lots of sandwiches and drinks. I especially remember they had baked bean sandwiches. I loved them so much I had never tasted anything like that before. I just kept going back till I ate all of them that day. It was the first time I had tasted baked-bean sandwiches.

Hercules was very patient with us and every night he would teach us a few words of English. Slowly we picked up enough English to use at school, but it was mainly schoolyard English. Neither the Government nor the school assisted us to learn the English language in those days. We either swam or sank. Eric went to night school and he learned 'Basic English' so he would also often sit with us in the evening and teach us the basic words as well. So slowly we learnt how to read and write. Hercules and Eric would both help us with our arithmetic and spelling homework. And later when we had various boarders who spoke English they would join in and help us with our homework. Among them were Charlie and Jim, two young men who actually worked at cafes in the evening. *Mama* was very strict with them and from the start had said to them, "You do not bring girls here, do you understand. This is a family home; you must respect this as your family home".

As the men all worked, *Mama* visited all the old second- hand shops and bought more cupboards and beds. She would drag me around the shops and with the little English I spoke she would get me to negotiate for the furniture. Often I felt the people must have felt sorry for me. And we would get the furniture for a good price.

I learnt to say "How much bed (or cupboard)?"They would tell us the price and then I would tell *Mama*. If it sounded too much she would tell me to say that it was too much. I would then say, "Too much, too much, better price please."

Mama put two single beds in the front room and we had two young men boarding with us, who had just arrived in Australia, Manolis and Theofanis. *Mama* also became a matchmaker for some of the tenants. For instance, she matched Manolis with *Thea* Mersina's oldest daughter, Anastasia. She then put another two single beds in the second room and we had another two men boarding with us. There were always new arrivals. As soon as some were able to save enough for a deposit they would go and buy their home. They all worked overtime and saved their money to buy a home. The rooms were never empty. As soon as some tenants left there were others who rented the empty room. It was a great income for us and it helped to pay the house off.

My brothers lived in the one bedroom and *Mama*, *Baba*, my sister and I shared the large room upstairs. In the tiny kitchen the boarders and we took turns to cook the meals and eat dinner at the one kitchen table. Then we would all sit out on the back patio or the upstairs front terrace and joke and laugh with each other telling stories of our day. Some would talk of the old country and how they missed their loved ones. That was our entertainment and then they went to their rooms to sleep.

There were at one time 10 adults and three children living in our house. We had a couple, Sofia and Dimitri, living with us and Dimitri's brothers, Thomas, Gianni and his sister, Arhodi. *Mama* was always ready to be a matchmaker for young people. She arranged for Thomas to meet *Thea* Mersina's second daughter, Chrissy. Thomas and Chrissy married on 2nd February, 1958. Family, friends and children attended the wedding. There was always dancing and lots of food at weddings; there were great celebrations for all of us. On the 17th April, 1959 they had a little girl, Anna. When she was baptised all family and friends celebrated the occasion.

When we all got together to celebrate occasions like *Baba's* Names' Day (St John's Day), *Baba*, (Gianni was now known as 'John'), or any other occasion it was a very enjoyable time for us kids as we had fun playing hide and seek or going to the park or to the beach. We all brought food and shared it and laughed and cried with each other, sharing our stories about settling into the new country.

The hardest part was when we all needed to go to the toilet at the same time and we would all line up and try to hurry each other, as some would take longer then usual, especially *Baba*. When I think about it, it was wonderful how we helped each other to make life a little easier for all of us, an incredible sharing and caring for each other. All those young men were migrants who had arrived to Australia, leaving behind their families and friends. By helping each other, it made life a little easier, as we had to learn the new language, the new culture and the different lifestyle.

We all laughed and cried with the different stories that were told each night. We had each other's shoulders to cry on. There was one story of one young man who stood on a lady's foot on the tram, so he had asked the others how to say *signomi* (sorry) in English in case it happened again. They told him he should say "shut up". The next day he had stood on the tram ticket conductor's foot and he had told the conductor "shut up" nice and loud. The conductor threw him off the tram and he wondered why. Well, all of them were in hysterics as they heard his story. They laughed and laughed as he told the story that evening. He saw the funny side of it when he found out that he should have said "sorry" instead of "shut up". He said that he would not trust any of them any more so he started night school to learn the English language with Eric.

Mama really liked to help, so she would volunteer me to help people find work or take them to the doctor's surgery. I would be their interpreter in my broken English. So early in the morning I would go with the different young men or ladies to various factories. We would knock on the doors of the factories and ask for work for the men. I especially remember one factory, Kia Ora, the fruit cannery, where I seemed to find work for many there. My English was really broken, but I would ask, "Have work for man? He good worker, do anything".

The men all thought I was fluent in the English language and were very thankful. *Mama* would tell them that I would always get the best price for the furniture. She was so proud of me. So guess what, if they wanted to buy anything they would take me along and I would get it for them.

Each time we had a new boarder *Mama* would be very strict with them and would repeat to each one, "No girls to come to your room, do you hear?" The agreement was that they each paid 30 shillings for the week. But while they each had to cook for themselves, *Mama* did their washing and changed their sheets weekly. The washing all went in the boiler in the laundry. Mama soaked it all and then washed and rinsed everything by hand in the twin cement tubs. That was how she helped *Baba* and my brothers in paying the house off.

As we slowly became better off financially, the front room was used as a lounge; *Mama* and I trotted back to the second-hand shop and bought some huge floral couches so that we were able to have visitors. The second-hand shop owner was used to us by now and when I would open my mouth to say "Too much money, please" he would say, "I know, I know, too much money, please".

By now most of our relatives had also migrated to Australia. *Thea* Taso and *Theo* Thanassos lived in Fitzroy, while *Thea* Ourania and *Theo* Christopher also lived in Fitzroy. *Theo* Parashos, *Thea* Mersina and all their children lived in Brunswick. *Theo* Stellios and *Thea* Chrissy were at Preston. These were all suburbs of Melbourne.

We loved visiting the various relatives and friends and we shared many stories and encouraged and helped each other. It was great, as each time there were Names' Days (or Saints' Days) of individuals there would be celebrations and dancing at the various homes. The women loved to cook and make the many sweets and various dishes of food. There was always dancing and singing and laughter, with the children playing hide and seek and lots of games.

Our outings were to go to church on a Sunday or visit the Botanical Gardens, the beach or the zoo and we would meet friends or relatives at those locations and enjoy a picnic with all of them. The women would bake and cook the various meals and we would all sit and share a banquet. We would also play a game of soccer or volleyball at the beach. I especially loved catching the tram to St Kilda Beach where we would go swimming or fish and often pick fresh mussels off the rocks. And in the evening we would go to Luna Park at St Kilda. The many rides were just wonderful and the room with many mirrors that made you look fat, skinny or short or the ghost train was so much fun.

The Olympic Games were being held in Melbourne in 1956 and we would have loved to go, but we could not afford the tickets. There was a competition on the radio to win a television set so I wanted to win one and I sent in my letter. I had to write who was the first European to land in Australia and what was the land called. I wrote my answer and sent it in and told them that it was the Dutch who called it Terra Australis. We were all thrilled when I won and *Mama* went to claim the prize, but we could only get half the value of a television set. You had to buy it for half price! So she then had to pay it off in instalments. But at least we were able to watch the Games from our television rather than look through the shop windows as many people did.

When the "Olympic Torch" came and it was to be taken into the stadium, we all went and watched the runner with the Torch. It was a great occasion for us as *Mama* said that great-grandma had come from Olympia where the original Olympics started. So I felt really proud of my name.

When our relatives came to visit us, we would go to the park and all the children would enjoy the slides and swings. Unfortunately, one day as my sister came down the slide the wrong way she ended up with a broken arm. We went to the doctor across the road and he sent her to the hospital. She had to have her arm in plaster for months and was not very happy about that.

Theo Christopher had sponsored *Giagia* Malamati and she lived with them for a while. But she could be annoying at times and *Theo* Christopher was pleased when she left to come to our home. So she ended up at our place for a while. Then after a time, she would go back to *Theo* Christopher's house when she wore out her welcome with us. This continued with *Giagia* Malamati moving back and forward between us. When *Giagia* moved in with us *Mama* had to have the back room vacant for her and had to ask the boarders to leave. *Mama* would often say "She is worse than a kid".

Tasoula and I had some colorful little tin turtle toys that my brother Hercules had bought for us when we arrived in Australia. We would put them on the fire mantelpiece and would enjoy playing with them. Their heads would move under their shells and it was a joy for us both. *Mama* would light the fires in the evening, as the rooms would get cold in winter and that was our heating for each room. Well, one day when we had left them on the mantelpiece, the toy turtles disappeared. We looked for them everywhere, but could not find them.

When *Mama* was cleaning the fireplace sure enough all those little turtles were found, but the color had been burnt off. We were not impressed so then *Mama* said to *Giagia*, "Did you throw the turtles into the fireplace *Giagia*?" "No! No! I would not do such a thing. No, I would not."

I was really angry and said, "Yes you did, when we went to bed you were the only one in the room when we left. You must have thrown them into the fire, *Giagia*".

She started giggling and said, "At night they moved, they really did. I had to stop them moving. I tell you there is something in this room that moves at night and it is scary. Whatever it is, it plays with the toys. I had to put a stop to that. So I threw the toys in the fire". We were not very happy with her. *Mama* was right; often she was worse than a kid.

Since *Giagia* moved in *Mama* decided to buy a washing machine. Washing by hand was really tiring for her, especially washing *Giagia's* thick, black clothes. Well that was something; we all celebrated when the "Stamco" wringer-type machine arrived. That was certainly a happy event for all of us. The first load was sheets and what a pleasure it was for *Mama* not to wash by hand in the cement tubs. We all stood around and watched the washing machine with fascination as the sheets went around and around in the washing machine and looked with wonder as *Mama* put the sheets through the wringer. She no longer had to wring clothes out by hand!

I then decided that I should try the wringer and put my hand through it. I tried to pull my arm out on my side of the washing machine and *Mama* kept on pulling it the other side. We were both trying to pull my arm from each side as it was being squashed. Suddenly I saw the lever and pulled it down and the wringer opened, thank God. *Mama* raced me to the doctor across the road. It was not broken, but badly bruised. *Giagia* was so impressed with the wringer; she too had to try the wringer the next day. Well, she also had her arm squashed and of course we all trotted back to the doctor again. We had become his best patients!

#34
Our Fish Shop

We were better off financially now, so my brothers, especially Eric, decided to open a fish shop. It was in a new area and in a block of seven little shops at Fairfield in a new industrial estate. This was a brand-new shop so it had to be fitted out with all the equipment. We all helped, but starting from scratch was hard work, as we had to fit it out and then build the business up.

We had no car and no-one could drive. To get to the shop we would catch a tram from Swan St down to Punt Road and then take a bus to Fairfield.

Eric had left Nielsons and he was running the fish shop by himself during the week while the rest of us helped at the weekends. Hercules had commenced his accountancy studies by correspondence from Canberra, so he was not able to help in the shop. But he did the entire bookwork for us. And any people who needed paperwork or taxation returns completed would come to my brother for help. *Mama* was really good at telling people that if they ever needed help with any paperwork Hercules, her son, could help them.

We could not afford to have people to deliver the potatoes and fish as it would be too costly. During the week *Baba* was working at GMH and I was at school. But early on Saturday mornings *Baba* and I would go to Victoria Markets at 5.00 am and do the purchasing for the shop. Because we had no car, we carried the fish, a sack of potatoes and chickens, which were often alive, on the tram. That was the only way we could afford to transport those items. All the passengers would stare at us. I was so embarrassed and felt like hiding under the seat each time, but I had to help my *Baba*. Whether I was a help or a hindrance only *Baba* knew. However, he enjoyed having me with him.

On the odd Saturday when we were early for the Markets we would go to the pictures to see Charlie Chaplin. *Baba* loved him and he would laugh his head off. It was a wonderful occasion when I would see him laugh so much.

Baba helped at the back of the shop peeling potatoes and cleaning the fish. Eric worked hard preparing the fish, the chips, cooking them and serving customers. If it was busy I would take the orders. When it was quiet I would help *Baba* peel the potatoes and cut the chips with a little machine into which we would put the peeled potatoes and then push the handle down and the chips would be cut. Everything was done by hand – no frozen food in those days. Eric would pre-cook the chips and prepare the fish so that when customers came in we were ready for them.

Although Eric was working hard and the business was slowly building up it was not bringing in enough to pay for the rent and for Eric's wages. We all sat down and agreed that it was not the right time for this business venture. Even though I was only 10 years old and had not been invited to join in the discussion I made sure that I was there. I loved it when we had the family discussions as we all tried to work out what was the best thing for all of us. As usual I enjoyed giving my opinion!

It amazes me now that with our limited knowledge of the English language, money being short and with no transport, we were prepared to have a go, to try our hand in business. It was all in God's timing, *Mama* said. This business venture was Eric's stepping stone, as he eventually had a very successful fish shop with his wife, Anna.

After working hard to build the business up for a few months we all were tired and, finding no financial reward, Eric sold the shop. Eric found work in the Dulux paint factory and worked with another man painting houses during the weekend. He was earning good money so he rewarded himself by buying his first watch and he gave me the watch that *Baba* had brought him from Switzerland. I was thrilled. I finally had a watch! He also brought a grey tabby kitten home that someone had left at the factory and we all loved it as it was very playful. It was wonderful to have a pet again. Eric named it Helvi.

Our lifestyle was improving and *Mama* decided that we should attend Greek school. She then enrolled us and we had to go to Greek school every Friday afternoon after we finished at our English school. I did not like the teacher as he always pulled my ear. One particular day the teacher asked me for the time as I was showing off my watch to other students, and talking, but I could not tell him the time in Greek. I had to do detention and he told me that I must not talk. Well, I liked the teacher even less after that. From then on I would try to avoid attending Greek school.

#35
The Weddings

Thea Sapfo had written to us to say that *Theo* George worked with a man who had a lovely daughter named Aspasoula. She thought that she would make a wonderful wife for Hercules, so she sent photos of her to him. Hercules sent photos of himself to Aspasoula and they started corresponding and eventually he sponsored her to migrate to Australia.

She came on the *Montserrat,* a Spanish boat, but on the way out it broke down and it took longer then usual to reach Australia. It arrived at Fremantle on the 10th June, 1959, so Hercules paid for her airfare to fly from Perth to Melbourne. Aspasoula arrived in Melbourne almost three weeks before the *Montserrat.* The boat did not get to Melbourne until the 29th June, 1959.

In the meantime Hercules was slack with his studies and his lecturer came to see us. Hercules was working at the Port Melbourne railway depot so he was not home when his lecturer called in to see him. *Mama* was happy when Tasoula and I arrived home from school so that I could interpret for her.

Mama had served him sesame cookies, coffee and a glass of cold water; they both sat across from each other, smiling, but unable to converse. As soon as we opened the door *Mama* called out to me,

"Olympia, this man is telling me something about Hercules, but I don't know what he is saying."

"*Mama,* you don't know him! How come you let him into the house?" I said to her, annoyed. I was upset that she would let a stranger into our home.

"He is trying to tell me something and he is showing me some papers. I do not understand him, but he is saying 'Hercules, Hercules'!"

I sat next to *Mama* and I said, "Can I help you, mister?"

"You can speak English, wonderful. I am Hercules' lecturer" the man said.

I looked at him puzzled as I did not know the meaning of the word 'lecturer' and said "lecturer?"

"I am sorry. I am his teacher at the college in Canberra, his correspondence school, and I was in Melbourne for some business. I have been sending letters, but Hercules has not answered. I thought I should pay him a visit to find out why he has not completed his lessons as he has nearly finished his course and all of a sudden he has not been sending any assignments in. He was doing so well and then he stopped. He is an excellent student and he will make a great accountant. He has great potential. He must not give up now as he has not long to go to finish his studies. I wondered what had happened to him."

The man talked slowly so I could understand as he realized that my English was limited.

I explained all of this to *Mama* and she was really pleased that the man had taken the time to come and enquire about Hercules.

Mama said to me, "Tell the man that Hercules has got engaged and his fiancée is travelling to Australia. When she arrives they will get married, but her boat has broken down, so he is really concerned that it is taking her so long to get here. Hercules cannot concentrate on his studies."

Mama was sure that that was the problem. I explained all that I could in my broken English, but the man understood. I was really pleased though when Hercules arrived and I then escaped and left them to it.

Hercules went on to finish his studies gaining distinctions for his subjects and we were all very proud of him. When Hercules applied for a job he got the first one he applied for and *Mama* was always very pleased that he worked in an office. He worked for the Health Department and he enjoyed it.

When Aspasoula's boat finally reached Fremantle in Western Australia, Hercules could not wait any longer and arranged for Aspasoula to fly from Perth to Melbourne. Hercules, *Mama* and *Baba* went to the airport to meet Aspasoula, taking a bunch of flowers with them for her.

When they came home they opened the door and Tasoula and I raced over and hugged Aspasoula. She was such a pretty person and she had a lovely laugh. We were thrilled to have an older sister. *Mama* was very strict and ensured that the wedding was arranged for the first of July, 1959.

A few days after her arrival *Mama* and all of us went to a bridal-wear hire shop where we tried on all the lovely dresses. Aspasoula looked beautiful in her wedding gown and my sister and I, with our cousin, Anna, were the bridesmaids. They got married at Saint Evagelismo Greek Orthodox Church at Victoria Parade, Melbourne.

The hall was hired and we prepared all the food for the wedding. All friends and their families were invited to the wedding. My brother's *koubarri* (best man) was Theodoros and his wife, Ebdoxia, was the lady-in-waiting. Their son held the candle for the bride and groom. That couple had come on the same boat to Australia as my brother. He often said to them "When I get married I would like you to be my best man". They had also worked together at the railway depot. We all loved celebrations, especially occasions such as weddings as in those days all our friends and relatives and children were invited. There was always lots of food and wonderful dancing as we all enjoyed kicking up our heels and we danced and danced.

There was no honeymoon for them. They lived in one of our bedrooms and Aspasoula settled into our home as if she had been with us all her life. We all loved her, as she was part of our family. *Mama* was very pleased to have Aspa as a daughter-in-law and she taught her to cook and keep house in a very encouraging manner.

Eric, who still worked with a man renovating, cleaning and painting houses on weekends as his second job, found a house at Oakleigh South, an outer suburb of Melbourne, and he wanted to buy it. We all sat down (again, including me at my own invitation), discussed it and decided that it would be great to buy the house.

By this time our English was much better so we caught the train to Oakleigh and then walked to South Oakleigh. *Mama*, Aspasoula, Tasoula and I and went to clean the house with all our cleaning gear again. This house was clean, but we still freshened it up and then we sat down and had a picnic on the steps and enjoyed the garden and the lovely fresh herbs that were growing there. We laughed and shared and enjoyed having the bigger yard for us to run and play. It had a "Hills" clothes hoist and we thought it was wonderful – it was our "merry-go-round". We loved having a ride on it as we hung on it and pushed each other round and round.

At the end of 1959 we moved to Oakleigh South and rented out the Richmond house. We hired a truck again; this time we had more furniture, but we all still hopped on to the truck as we relocated to our new home. *Mama*, *Baba*, Hercules, Aspasoula, Eric, Tasoula, me and the cat Helvi all moved into our new home. *Mama* said we must put butter on the feet of the cat so she would not get lost in this place, but unfortunately this did not work and Helvi did get lost. Although we all searched for him throughout the neighbourhood we could not find Helvi.

We all loved this home as there was a lovely garden and the home was not as old as the terraced Richmond home.

Eric still worked at the Dulux paint factory, which was at Huntingdale, during the week and on weekends he worked renovating houses with another man. Aspasoula worked at a factory in Oakleigh where they made plastic bottles. *Baba* was the one who had to travel by train and bus, but as he worked afternoon shift the bus would drop him at the corner of Warrigal Road and Dandenong Road., and he would then have to walk for at least an hour and a half, as he still worked at GMH at Port Melbourne.

My sister and I started school at Oakleigh South Primary. I loved all sports, but not schoolwork and I was picked for the school basketball team. I was thrilled to be in the team, but when I was also chosen to be the captain of the team I was so excited. But I had a problem as my English was not the best and as the captain, when we played against another school I had to ask the vice-captain, whose name was Gerhart (her parents were Dutch), to thank the other school team.

Mama, for the first time, did not have boarders to look after, but she still had to cook, wash and iron for all of us. She loved cooking and would often exchange recipes with *Theas*, especially for various sweets. This house had a lovely big stove and *Mama* enjoyed cooking on it as she had only to light it. It was a gas stove and she did not have to go looking for coins to cook. When we came home from school the house had a beautiful aroma from her cooking, as she was always trying new recipes that *Thea* Mersina or *Thea* Taso had given to her. And *Baba* was in his glory as he planted lots of vegetables and fruit trees. We always had fresh vegetables from the garden.

We had family and friends often visit us or we would visit them, and shared all the fruit and vegetables with each other. *Baba's* tomatoes were the best-tasting ones I had ever eaten and often neighbours and friends were supplied as well. This sharing between each other was our strength and encouragement in our new country.

Hercules and his friends who had worked together at the railway depot always kept in touch and often went with Theodoros and Ebdoxia and their son, Stellios, to watch the soccer on Saturday afternoons. Now and then Hercules would take me along but he would get embarrassed as I would scream and yell while he just sat and watched the game.

Thanassis and Despina Rovolidis with their new baby daughter, and some of his other friends, with whom he worked at the railway depot, would visit us on Friday evenings. We would all watch *Bonanza* in the TV as they did not have a TV We all enjoyed each other's company.

It was now Easter time. Aspa was pregnant and instead of *Bonanza* we were all watching the *Passion of Christ* and Jesus was cooking fish by the lake. Aspasoula said, "It's incredible I can smell the fish". Then *Mama* jumped up and yelled, "Oh my goodness, I had put a big pot of fresh corn to cook and I think it's burnt". It certainly was burnt, but we all laughed and laughed.

My parents sponsored my *Thea* Sapfo, *Theo* George and my cousins Spiro and Kostas to Australia. We found them a house to rent close by and *Thea* found work at a nursing home as a nurse.

It was wonderful to have them close by, especially for *Mama*, as they were the only relatives she had in Australia. My cousins Spiro and Kostas went to our school. In the summertime we all would catch the bus to Mordialloc and have a wonderful time together having picnics by the beach.

Our yard was big enough for us all to play in and Spiro and Kostas were great to have with us and often we would play Robin Hood and his merry men or Superman. On one of these occasions I wanted to be Superman. Tasoula said, "Don't be silly, you can't be Superman".

I yelled at he, "Of course I can". I stood on the edge of my bed and leaped to catch on to the ledge above the door to our bedroom. The ledge came falling down on my head, bricks and all. *Mama* was furious as this was Eric's house and what would he say as I had destroyed it with my jump? So she started belting me; I was really annoyed and yelled at her, "You are not my mother! *Thea* Anna is my mother; all you do is belt me!"

"What did you say? Olympia, say that again!"

She was furious and so was I. I did not say it again. But she belted me again. *Baba* heard the yelling and he come to see what had happened. When he saw what had happened he had a grin on his face and I was pleased.

"Leave her alone. She just has lots of spirit," he said.

"Lots of spirit? Look what she has done. It is Eric's house and you think it is funny! She could have killed herself if the brick had hit her on the head."

"Thank God she is all right. St George was sure looking after her again," *Baba* said, and grinned at me. When Eric came home he was really good about it and he and *Baba* fixed the wall.

Aspa, who was pregnant, worked until the ninth month. She said that she felt good and did not mind working, plus she did not show that she was pregnant. My first niece, Olga, named after *Mama*, was born on the 28th of June, 1960 to Aspa and Hercules at Oakleigh Hospital. We were all thrilled and naturally we spoilt her. And we often fought over who would nurse her and take her for a walk in the pram.

My parents had bought a block of land at Knoxfield and *Baba* told us that "it is only down the road", so one Sunday morning all the family decided to walk from Oakleigh South to Knoxfield to look at the block of land. We thought it would be a great opportunity to also pick wild greens to cook and eat. We would clean the greens, then put some water in a saucepan with some salt, bring it to the boil and then place the greens in the boiling water and cook them for five minutes. We would then drain them and serve the greens with salt, oil and lemon.

Although we still had no car we all decided it would be great to go and have a picnic and look at the block. It would take half an hour to drive there by car, so it was a long walk. We also had baby Olga in the pram and we walked and laughed and walked and walked. We had left very early in the morning and we got there by lunchtime. We found the block of land at 20 Phillip Road Knoxfield where we had our picnic and picked wild greens.

After lunch we packed up and then headed for home. It was not hard going down Ferntree Gully Road as at Wheelers Hill there is a huge hill that we walked down, but when we had to go uphill pushing a pram, it was hard. We all took turns to push the pram, but it was getting dark and we were all getting tired by now. *Baba* kept saying "It's not far now". He loved walking and he could keep going, but the rest of us were really tired, so I started to use the sign to hitchhike, but drivers would not stop.

At last a small truck stopped and asked us where we wanted to go. I told him we lived at Oakleigh South, but if he could just drop us corner of Warrigal and Dandenong roads we would appreciate it. The driver said, "The women and the children can hop on the truck". *Mama* sat in the front seat holding the baby and Aspa, Tasoula and I got on to the back of the truck. We folded the pram and put it with us on the back of the truck. We all had to hold on to the rail at the back of the driver's cabin as there were no sides to the truck. *Baba*, Eric and Hercules walked home.

Baba would catch the train to Port Melbourne GMH where he often met another man, Hlia Kapsis, who would catch the train at Bentleigh and together they would talk and they found out that Hlia Kapsis came from Florina and *Baba* came from Tropaioukhos, near Florina. The friendship was built and Hlia Kapsis said that he had lovely daughters and my *Baba* said he had an eligible son, Eric. We started visiting each other and then they arranged for Eric and his daughter, Anna, to get to know each other. They had their engagement in November 1961.

We enjoyed visiting Anna's family as our family was growing with all the extended relatives. It was just wonderful. Anna had three sisters and a younger brother, Taki, who went to technical school. Her two older sisters were married with young children. The older sister, Souli, was married to Paul and had two children, Jim and Martha. The second sister, Thelma, and her husband Paul also had two children, Susie and Chris. Anna and her younger sister, Rina, both worked in Malvern at "Ezi Walking" shoe store. Rina was my age and I thought that if she was working I should try and find work as well. It would be good if I could find a part-time job after school or on Saturday mornings for pocket money.

When I saw an advertisement in the local paper that Coles wanted staff for Saturday mornings I thought it would be great to apply to earn pocket money, but we had to apply by the end of the week. So when Eric came home I told him and he said that it was fine and that he would come with me. I was not allowed to go by myself so he had to escort me, but we had no car and we had to ride our bikes to the shops. We were having a race and both rode our bikes as fast as we could. As we were coming around a corner to take a turn to go up over the bridge, Eric's bike hit the high gutter and his bike's front wheel buckled up and he was thrown over the handlebars. He fell and grazed his knees. I think it was his pride more bruised than his knees, as he had to carry his bike home.

I went on to apply for the job alone, but I was hot from riding my bike and upset because of Eric's accident, so the interview did not go well when I saw the manager and I did not get the job.

Anna and Eric married on the 10th of June, 1962 in the Greek Church at Victoria Parade. The church was called Saint Evagelismo, the same church where Hercules and Aspasoula had married. It is one of the oldest Greek Orthodox churches in Melbourne. We invited all the relatives and friends. It was a big wedding and this time we had the people at the reception hall catering for the wedding.

Thea Sapfo said to my *Mama,* "Have you had a chat to Eric about his first night of marriage?" *Mama* was very surprised and said, "No one told Gianni and me what we had to do when we got married, they can find out themselves, I am not going to tell him". So *Thea* sat down and had a chat to Eric before the wedding. Eric and Anna went on their honeymoon to Mildura, but they worked picking grapes and earn money while on their honeymoon! Eric was always a very hard worker.

The house at 55 Golf Road, South Oakleigh was too small for all of us so Aspa and Hercules, *Thea* Sapfo and Theo George, Spiro and Kosta moved to the house at Richmond. *Mama* looked after baby Olga during the week and then Aspa and Hercules would have her on the weekend. *Mama* often suffered with migraine headaches and she would wind a scarf around her head to relieve her pain. We knew then not to trouble her. This helped *Mama* as she had to rest if she had her migraine, so Eric always helped. Eric would get up during the night when Olga cried. He would warm the milk, feed her and change her nappy, or often I would help if baby Olga cried. Looking after the baby during the week helped both Aspa and Hercules to go to work. Often I would go and stay with them on the weekend and loved babysitting Olga. My cousin Anna helped Aspa to find work at Hiltons, the stocking factory, when they moved back to Richmond. It was not unusual for friends and relatives to find work for each other.

I started working on a Saturday at "Ezi Walking" with Anna and Rina and I enjoyed my Saturday morning work. It also meant I had pocket money. The shop next to "Ezi Walking" was a Chinese restaurant. When I was taking the empty boxes out the back I saw a cat that had kittens next-door and I was admiring them. My boss Charlie come behind me and said to me, "You know that they will eat these cats. They eat cats you know".

When he left, I thought to myself '*At least one cat would not be eaten, I am taking it home*'. So I put a little kitten in an empty shoebox and took it home. Its eyes were not fully opened yet and when I took it home *Mama* said, "Olympia, what would you do with a kitten so young? It still needs its mother".

"*Mama*, I could not leave the kitten there. My boss said that those people eat the cats. I had to save it."

"He was just teasing you. People do not eat cats these days. Yes, during the wars when there is no food people have been known to eat cats, but not here."

I went looking and found a little doll's milk bottle and I then started feeding the kitten every two hours. I made a small bed for it and put it in the laundry corner. It was a tough little kitten and grew to be a wonderful cat. As I was still going to school, I had *Mama* feed the little kitten every two hours, until I came home. We called that cat Spots as it had a black spot on its nose. She was a black and white playful kitten and we all loved her.

My cousins Spiro and Kosta and *Theo* George had brought home to our place a lovely dog, a red setter, which they had found. Living at Richmond the house hardly had any yard so they brought the dog to us at Oakleigh South. It was great to have a dog again, but it loved wandering around and often would jump the fence and bring home plates or milk bottles or what ever it could find. Next-door we had a charming Italian family and often *Mama* and the Italian lady would talk over the fence and exchange food. One would hand over Italian food and the other Greek food. Just as *Mama* looked after Olga, her granddaughter, the Italian lady also had her two grandchildren to look after. She would sit outside to feed her grandchildren and then the plates would be left outside as she went in to put the grandchildren down for their afternoon nap. Our wonderful dog was great. He would go and bring the plates to our house and the neighbour would yell that our dog had taken the dishes again.

Red, as we called him, was beautiful, but he did not like being tied up and would bark whenever tied up. But then if we left him loose, it did not take him long to jump the fence and collect whatever he could find in the neighbours' places. The neighbours started complaining and so *Baba* decided to take the dog to Dandenong to a friend's farm. He caught the train with the dog and then left him at the farm. By the time *Baba* was back at home the dog was already at our place. *Baba* did that a couple of more times with the same result. But in the end he found people who had children and he said that when he left Red he looked at him with big, brown eyes as if to say 'You're leaving me again'. However, this time Red stopped at the farm.

#36

We move to Oakleigh

Travelling was getting too much for *Baba*. Eric had been renovating a house so that the owner could sell it. He said that it would probably sell at a reasonable price. We went to the estate agent who had the house on the market and he took us all to see the house. It was only five minutes walk to the railway station, and *Baba* would not have to walk for over an hour and a half every night to get home. *Mama* was not sure if they should go into debt. But *Thea* Sapfo said to her, "Olga, you have always wanted your own home. This is your opportunity. The home is cheap and it is close to the shops, trains and buses".

We all then went and saw the house again; it was an old timber home with two bedrooms, a lounge and dining room, a tiny kitchen, bathroom and laundry. The lounge and dining rooms were separated with a sliding door.

We discussed whether or not we should buy the house. Naturally, I gave my opinion!

Baba and *Mama* bought it for £3000, but they only had enough for a deposit so they went to the bank and got a loan. We all got together and Eric painted the house inside and we cleaned it and moved in. *Mama* was very thankful that she at last had her own home. *Baba* was thrilled as he had a shed and he started planting lots of fruit trees and had a lovely vegetable garden again, and a little henhouse. He bought some hens and we had our own fresh eggs. He planted roses at the front and when the first rose opened he brought it to *Mama* and she put it in a vase.

Mama and *Baba* had the front bedroom and Tasoula and I had the lounge room as our bedroom. We used the dining room as our lounge and simply closed the sliding door. We rented the back bedroom to a couple and *Mama* looked after Olga, and a little boy next-door, Robert.

Tasoula and I caught the bus to high school as we attended Huntingdale High. I loved playing sport, but still did not like schoolwork that much. I thrived and enjoyed all kinds of sport, from athletics, basketball, hockey and softball. Tasoula was more conscientious and did better at schoolwork. But I must admit I did enjoy Art. I had an assignment for Art and I was given a block of plaster of paris and we had to sculpture an animal or whatever we wished. I found tools at Baba's shed and sat it on a table outside and tried to sculpture a donkey. *Baba* was working in his vegetable patch as he often did and he saw me that I was having trouble using a chisel and he joined me and said, "Olympia, what are you trying to do?" I said, "*Baba,* I would like to chisel the donkey we had in the village, but I am not very successful". He then went and bought a little saw and then the two of us chiseled and sawed. While we worked on my Art assignment we talked about our animals that we had in the village and he would tell me of his life growing up at Kouvouklia and how mischievous he would be as a young child and the fun he had with his brother and cousins. He would tell me how he loved being in his garden as he enjoyed growing things and that was where he found God in his garden, as he saw things growing. He just loved nature

As he was telling me about his childhood I asked him, "*Baba,* you only go to church on special occasions such as your 'Names' Day'. How come?"

He smiled and tilted his head and was silent for a while. 'Olympia, to please your *Mama...*" Then he continued, "Olympia, when I was very young I was an altar boy". I interrupted him saying, "*Baba,* you were an Altar Boy? Whooo!"

"Yes I was an altar boy every Sunday. I would help the old priest at Kouvouklia. He was a very good priest when he was young, but when people were persecuted for their faith, only old ladies attended to light candles as people were afraid to go to church. This old priest would sit and drink the wine and get drunk. He would then get angry and swear and yell at me when I helped him. So I promised myself not to swear and I knew that God lived in my heart and in nature. I can see that everywhere as I only have to look at the beautiful flowers."

"*Baba,* you had lost everything, leaving your home in Turkey, then the war in Greece. I often wonder why you do not talk about the war, do you? There must be painful memories for you".

"Olympia my child, you ask too many questions. I hate wars and violence. When Christopher lost his finger in the accident at General Motors they called me to the sick bay, as I was his brother. When I saw his fingers hanging and the blood I fainted. They did not know who to look after, me or Christopher. I am not the best with blood. I had seen enough in my life. I hate wars and violence and suffering. I know that I was proud to fight for my country. We had a job to do and we did it. They are not the best of memories; they are memories to be left behind".

Times like that I cherished as *Baba* was not much of a talker, so whatever we shared I treasured. I actually got top marks for the little donkey that we sculpted together and it was put in display in the art room. It meant a lot to me as I had shared time with *Baba*.

I loved working with Anna, my sister-in-law, as she was like an older sister to me. At "Ezi Walking" shoe shop at Malvern, Anna worked as a saleslady and her sister Rina worked in the office. I worked in the children's department on Saturday mornings as a saleslady. It was very enjoyable and I loved working there. Tasoula started working there at "Ezi Walking" as well, but she did not like it and she then started working in the fruit shop around the corner from where we lived. At least those jobs provided us with our pocket money and we did not have to worry *Mama* and *Baba* for that. Although we had our own pocket money there was not enough for the extras we needed.

I loved playing hockey and I was asked to join the Victorian women's hockey team, but my parents did not have enough money to pay for the uniforms and hockey sticks that I needed. I could borrow a hockey stick from my school, but I could not do that all the time. I asked *Mama*, "*Mama*, do you think you could help me by buying me a uniform and a hockey stick? I have been invited to join the Victorian women's hockey team."

She said, "Olympia, Olympia, young ladies do not go chasing a ball with the stick. You have to learn the art of housekeeping and needlework and possibly go on and become a school teacher and get married".

"*Mama,* I do not like school work. I'd rather play hockey! Please, will you help me?"

She was annoyed and said, "Olympia, your *Baba* is working extra overtime and I am looking after kids and we rent the one bedroom to pay the house off. How can we afford to pay for the extras you are asking for?"

She went and started a cross-stitch mat for me to embroider and she said, "Olympia, learn to be a good housekeeper rather than chase a ball". She sat down and showed me how to do cross-stitch (Over 50 years later I still have that unfinished mat!)

Our chores were that every Saturday morning Tasoula and I had to clean the house and polish the furniture before we went to work. While we did that we would have the Beatles or Elvis songs playing and we would rock and roll doing the housework. *Mama* did not think that was very ladylike. Then on Sundays we had to do the cooking to make sure that we would be good housekeepers when we got married. She was very concerned that we were well groomed in running a home. *Mama* taught us the art of housekeeping such as making filo pastry, or baking various pitas and dishes.

But when poor *Mama* was suffering from migraines she would have to lie down. I would help with the cooking. *Mama* had bought a pressure cooker and she loved cooking all these wonderful stews. So I thought I would cook spaghetti in the pressure cooker, but I had put too much water and the stove on high and then the lid blew and the spaghetti all stuck on the ceiling. I thought it was so funny, but *Mama* was not very impressed with me at all.

On Sundays we would often have a roast chicken that *Mama* would kill from our own chickens, so that I would then prepare it and cook it. First I needed to pluck its feathers by putting it into the boiling water for a few minutes in a saucepan and then pulling its feathers out. I would then have to clean it and then take all its gizzards out then cook it with potatoes in the oven. On some Sundays we would have a leg of lamb, so I would baste it and put garlic into it, and rub onion and all herbs over the leg. I would then either squeeze some lemon on it or cook it with homemade salsa. I did enjoy cooking and did not mind the housekeeping either, as when we did that we would have the records playing and Tasoula and I would dance as we did housework.

I lost interest in schoolwork and would not concentrate. At the end of the year I told *Mama* that I was not going back to school so she went and saw the bank manager and asked him if he wanted people to work for him. She made an appointment for me to see him. For the interview I went to put on the nice clothes that I wore at "Ezi Walking" shoe shop when working on Saturdays and holidays. *Mama* said, "Olympia, wear your school uniform to show that you are respectable young lady".

"But *Mama,* I am going for a job interview. I have to dress nicely."

Mama yelled, "Would you for once listen to me? I know what I am saying."

So the two of us went off to see the bank manager, *Mama* and me, with me wearing my school uniform. I even had to wear my school hat and my gloves!

The bank manager's name was Mr Rodd. He was a very nice person and an understanding one. He gave me all the forms to fill out and then when I did them he said I could start as he needed someone who could speak Greek, as he had lots of Greek customers. He told me that I would need to go into Melbourne to have a medical examination first and if it was successful I could start before the Christmas rush.

I told Mr Rodd that I had finished all my Grade 10 school exams in early November and that I could start work in the bank at the end of November. I was not sure how well I had done in my exams. He said, "That is all right, I'll take the last term's report card if you can bring that along next time". And then he looked at my *Mama* and at me and he said, "Olympia, when you go for your examination, wear some nice clothes, shoes, stockings and maybe a little lipstick on, is that all right with you, *Mama*?" And he looked at *Mama*. I felt like jumping up and down with joy but I kept a straight face.

The next day *Mama* came home with a deep red lipstick and a dress that was white with black spots. I actually loved the dress, which I wore to the medical examination and I put on a touch of lipstick. I started work at the end of November 1963 in the Bank of New South Wales. I worked as ledger machinist and also did interpreting for loans or for any overseas transactions that people needed. I had to go to the Head Office in Melbourne for my training.

I enjoyed working in the bank during the week. On the weekend I continued to work on Saturday mornings at the "Ezi Walking" shop and then visit Hercules and Aspa in the afternoon. We would often go to the pictures on Saturday afternoons. On one particular Saturday we all went to the Greek pictures. There were *Mama*, Tasoula, Aspa, *Thea* Sapfo and her sons, Spiro and Kostas, and me. The movie was a sad one and all of us were crying when it had finished. But *Mama* collapsed on a seat as she had an angina attack. Thank God we had *Thea* Sapfo with us, as she was a nurse and helped us. We then went to the doctor and *Mama* was diagnosed with a bad heart and from then on she would often have angina or heart attacks and would end up at the hospital. But she still continued looking after children and having tenants living in the house.

Since I now was working fulltime in the Bank, *Mama* would volunteer Tasoula to help neighbours and friends with interpreting as they could not speak the language. She would go with them to their doctor or solicitor and interpret for them. We had a lovely young couple, Sofia and Gianni, living with us, who came from Rhodes and could not speak a word of English. They were renting a room from us. They were expecting their first child and every month when Sofia needed to go to the doctor either Tasoula or I would take her. Our *Mama* would volunteer us to help them or anyone else who needed an interpreter.

Baba came home from work one day with really swollen feet and legs. It was very unusual for him to stay at home. But he was not well as he had a clot and he had to stay in bed for a long time. *Mama* and I struggled to make the loan repayments and have food on the table. Even though *Baba* had been working at GMH for a long time there was no help from them. He was feeling really sick at work so he had told the boss he had to go home, but he did not tell the boss that he was sick. He had left work that day and had not told them what the problem was so they put it down that it did not happen at work.

Mama had taken in more children to look after. She had Olga, Robert, Sandra and Helen and with me working in the bank and on Saturdays at "Ezi Walking" shoe shop we managed to keep making the payments and we paid off the block of land that *Baba* and *Mama* had at Knoxfield. *Mama* said to me, "Do not tell anyone that we are just making ends meet" as we were struggling. We would sit down and count the money and then pay our bills. Tasoula was still going to high school and *Mama* and I did not tell her or anyone else that we were struggling. My wage was not high, but between us we managed to pay all our bills. My brothers did not know the hardship that we were going through at the time.

At this time we also received a letter from my *Thea* Giannoula asking us to go back to Greece as squatters were claiming the house and lands that *Mama* and *Baba* had worked so hard for in Greece. We did not have the money for my parents to go back to Greece, so the property in Greece was taken over by the squatters. *Baba* often said, "It was who you knew in the village that mattered, as the local government people distributed properties to friends and family". My parents lost all they had once again and all the hard work that they had put into it for years was lost. Even though they had documents that showed that they had paid for everything, the local government accepted the people who lived there and gave them ownership. My parents were devastated when they lost everything again.

As soon as *Baba* was all right he started back at GMH and he enjoyed his work. One day he came home and he was annoyed. Then he said, "We are getting Turkish migrants to work with us now. There was a young Greek man at work who started picking on an old Turkish man. I grabbed the young man and shook him for doing that. I said to him, 'How dare you do that to the man? He too has left his country and family to come and better himself, as we all have.' He had no right to do that. What does he know of losing loved ones? I had lost my father, sister, homes and land and I should have hatred towards this man as I was a refugee from Turkey. But how can I do that to the man, as wars are not created by the ordinary people and they are the ones that suffer. As I have suffered so has this man suffered. He has come to make a better life for himself and his family just as I have. We do not bring hatred to this land. Forgiveness is the only answer to hatred. For people like him and us this is our *Promised Land*."

I just sat and listened. *Baba* did not often voice his opinion but when he did he made lots of sense.

Once *Baba* settled back into work they saved enough to extend the tiny kitchen and laundry and to put a toilet in the bathroom. It took a while to get it finished as the builder was working on other sites.

My cat Spots that I had brought home from "Ezi Walking" was pregnant and ready to have her kittens. I would sneak her into our bedroom at night-time as I felt sorry for her being outside and she would sleep with me. During the night I was fast asleep and suddenly the cat was biting my hand and I woke up to find that she was having her kittens on my bed in the middle of the night. I had on the bed a flookate blanket (a long-haired blanket) and my cat was having her kittens on my bed. Slowly someone opened the door and stuck their head in our room, to see what was happening; it was *Baba,* who had come home from work. It was just after midnight as he was working late shift and he saw a light in our room so he opened to see what was happening and he saw me delivering the kittens. He whispered, "Olympia, your *Mama* will kill you. She is not going to be happy with you. Look at the blanket, it is full of blood. You were not to bring your cat inside; she was to have stayed in the shed".

I looked at *Baba* with pleading eyes and said, "I could not leave Spots outside, *Baba*, she is in pain. She woke me so that I could help her, aren't her kittens beautiful?" She had five beautiful kittens and she was cleaning them. "Come, we better put the blanket in the wash, put the cat in a box with her kittens and put her in the shed before your *Mama* wakes up." *Baba* went and fetched a box from the shed and I found some old rags and we put the kittens in and the cat hopped into the box. "*Baba,* we can't put her in the shed, she will get cold. Can't we just put her in the laundry please," I pleaded. We put them in the laundry and closed the door and then put the thick blanket in the bathtub, filled it with water and then I just trod on the blanket to wash it, rinsed it a few times and then hung it up with the help of *Baba*. Washing that thick blanket was not easy. I jumped on it and jumped on it. *Mama* was not very happy when she found out the next day and I was in trouble again!

The kittens grew and they were beautiful, but *Mama* said I had to get rid of all of them and only keep the little male as it looked like Spots. "*Mama,* you can't do that. I love Spots. She is beautiful and she is a great mother."

"No you have to get rid of them all except the little male." She got Hercules who had a friend Jim with a car and they went and dumped my cat. I was really upset. Hercules said that Spots looked at him when he did that and he felt terrible.

I then had to give the kittens away. I searched and searched looking for attractive houses. I figured if their houses were neat they would be lovely people. I knocked at their door and then ran, but had left them each a adorable kitten. I watched from the side as each person took the kitten and I was very happy and prayed that they would love and look after the kitten.

Anna and Eric were expecting their first child and we were really happy for them. Then on the 10th of November, 1964 their twins, Maria and Debbie, were born. We were all really excited to have new nieces. My parents were thrilled to have three lovely granddaughters, Olga (Aspa's and Hercules'daughter), and now the twins, Maria and Debbie, (Eric's and Anna's daughters). We loved visiting them to nurse the twins. The family was growing and my parents were thrilled to have grandchildren. They felt very blessed having grandchildren.

#37

Giagia Malamati moves in with Us

My cousin Anna had married John Paioff in Perth and all the rest of the family, *Theo* Christopher, *Thea* Ourania and their children moved to Perth. So *Giagia* Malamati was back with us again! But we had tenants in the room, so she moved in with Tasoula and me in our bedroom.

In the meantime *Mama* had sponsored my cousin, Thomas Kostandinidis, her sister's (Giannoulla's) son, so he migrated to Australia. We put a single bed in our lounge and he stayed with us. We had a full house again, and we had the large hall between kitchen and bathroom and laundry as our lounge room. *Mama* had put the television set in the corner with our couches in this hallway. In the evening we all sat watching the shows, and *Giagia* demanded each time to watch the animal shows. *Mama* liked the various serials and Tasoula and I wanted the musicals, quiz shows or rock and roll shows, so there would be friendly arguments every night to see which show would be the best to watch.

We often had *Giagia's* brother Parashos visit us. As we came around the corner from the side of the house we would hear the two of them arguing politics. *Giagia* was always dressed in black with a black scarf and she would often sit out on the front patio and enjoyed waving at people when they went past our home. She enjoyed the peace and the sunshine and sometimes she would sit at the back and watch the free-range chickens pecking away. She often said to us, "This place is so peaceful; we can at last sleep in peace and not worry about wars and hunger". But then she would advise us, "Make sure you always have a good supply of salt, sugar, soap and matches, as these were the things that we missed often when we had war".

Hercules, Aspa, *Thea* Sapfo and *Theo* George lived together at Richmond, but they were getting unsettled. *Thea* and *Theo* wanted to return back to Greece. When they came to see us they would say "life in Australia was all concentration on work and home. There was no quality of life as we all worked hard to pay off our houses". *Thea* Sapfo told us that they missed the lifestyle in Greece, where after work they would go to the restaurants or walk along the promenade along the shores of Thessaloniki. *Theo* George refused to work in Australia as he felt we all worked like slaves and he was not prepared to do that, so he stayed at home and did the housekeeping while *Thea* worked.

Mama often said to my *Thea,* "How can your husband do the washing, especially your pants? That's terrible". *Thea* would laugh and say, "Olga, Olga, times have changed, there is nothing wrong with George picking up the kids and doing the cooking. I cannot do both jobs. At least he makes himself useful as I have to work to pay the bills". She continued working as a nurse in nursing homes.

The house next-door was being sold so my cousin Thomas bought it; at last we had our lounge back. As the hall lounge was cold in the winter we used a portable kerosene heater that *Mama* or *Baba* lit very early in the morning, but that did not heat the entire house. The kerosene heater was moved between kitchen and lounge.

Hercules came to us in June and said to my parents that Aspa and he had decided to go back to Greece. They put the house on the market and got all their furniture packed and were going back to Greece by boat in October. My *Thea* Sapfo and *Theo* George with our cousins Spiro and Kosta were all going back as well. My brother had found a good job in Greece and he was really pleased that they would have a better lifestyle there.

Our church was having a dinner dance at Oakleigh and all of the family was going. My brother had had all his vaccinations and he was not really well, but as it was going to be a family celebration we all went. We all sat around enjoying each other's company and then Hercules danced with me. When that dance finished he was heading to ask Aspa to dance with him. As we were going back to our table a young man approached me and asked me to dance. I felt so honored that someone had asked me to dance with them, and I enjoyed dancing with him. For him to ask me that night I felt on cloud nine. All his family attended our church and I must admit that in later times I often went to church with *Mama* to see if he was there. However, when I went back to the table my *Baba* reprimanded me, as the young man had not come to ask his permission so that I could dance with him. I said, "*Baba,* that is Bill, one of our church people, and we know all his family". That really spoilt my night. My parents were strict and I respected them, but I felt it was, after all, a church function and everyone knew each other. And I did have a crush on Bill for a long time, but I had never told anyone about it.

The day arrived when we had to say our goodbyes as Hercules, Aspa and Olga were leaving. *Mama* and *Baba* were devastated that their oldest son was leaving and going back to Greece.

Baba said to Hercules "My son, *Na Xeris Dio Patrithes ine thiskola* (to know two fatherlands is hard); to know which one is better and to choose where to live is not an easy thing. But my son, I know one thing, that this land has given us the freedom and the peace of mind, we can eat a piece of bread in peace, without the worry that soldiers will come and kill us. This is our home; this is our *Promised Land* where there is peace and freedom. I wish you well, my son, and hope that you will find happiness and joy in your journey. *H Dunami Tou Theou na Ine pandode mazi sou* (May God's strength be always with you), that was my *Baba's* blessing. May this blessing carry you too".

There were lots of tears and hugs as we farewelled them at Port Melbourne.

#38

Tonsillitis and My Wedding

After Aspa and Hercules left it was very hard for *Mama* as she loved Olga and she was not there any more. She missed her oldest granddaughter. There was a void for all of us, but we were thankful we had the twins and that was a joy for my parents and for all of us.

I was continuing to get a sore throat and so the doctor told me that I should have my tonsils out. I enjoyed working at the bank, but because I was missing work every now and then (because of my throat), I realised I should get them out. I was working at "Overseas Transactions" where an Italian man and his son often came into the bank for the father's pension. When I was helping them one day the young man said to me, "My father really likes you and I think you're nice. I wondered if you would like to go out with me, Olympia".

I felt honoured and pleased that someone would even think of asking me out, but I knew my parents were really strict, so I thought I had better tell them the truth and said, "Thank you for asking me out. I feel honoured, but you would need to come and ask my father if it's all right for me to go out with you, as my parents are really strict".

From then on the father came on his own into the bank to get his pension, as the son probably did not want to ask my father. I did not blame him.

A couple of weeks later Bill walked into the bank. He was the young man who had asked me to dance at the church dinner. I noticed he wanted to speak to me so I went over to the counter and said to him "Can I help you?" It must have been hard for him as he was not sure what to say and he first coughed a dry cough and then said, "Olympia, I would like to take you out". I was so thrilled as I did have a crush on him, but I said, "Sorry, I cannot go out with you as I am not allowed to go out". He looked at me and then coughed and moved his head slightly and again said, "I just want to talk to you. We will only just walk on the street". Even though I was thrilled, I felt I knew I would not be allowed and simply said, "Sorry, I can not go out with you". He left and he looked so hurt I wanted to rush after him and say that I would love to go out with him, but I am not allowed as my parents are strict. I still don't know why I did not do that.

I was away again for a week with tonsillitis and running a temperature, before I went back to work. The date was set for me to go to Saint Cabrini Hospital to have my tonsils out.

I was working at the counter when a young man who had lost a cheque a few weeks ago was back in the bank to send money to his parents in Crete. His name was Nikolaos and he was pleased that I was back as he had come in the week before when I had been away.

He said, "It is good you are back. I could not understand what they were saying to me last week".

I served him with his transactions and then I said to him "I will be away again as I am having my tonsils out next week".

When I went in to hospital to have my tonsils out the nurse told me, "There is a patient in the next room. He is Greek".

The next day when I was in bed the nurse brought the patient from the next room over to see me as he had had an operation and was going home. He had some Greek magazines and thought that I might like to read them. When she brought him over I knew him as he was a customer of the bank. His name was Andrew. I could not talk too much, but we shook hands and greeted each other and I never thought of it again.

When I got home from the hospital I was really hungry and even though the doctor had said to me "only ice-cream and jelly for a few days", *Mama* had grilled some lovely lamb chops, which were my favorite food, and made a big salad. I decided I was well enough to enjoy a nice chop and gulped it down. During the night I was choking and I started splattering. Tasoula woke up and called out to *Mama* that I had blood flowing out of my mouth. They called our Doctor Ludbrook and when he came he said,. "Olympia, you have just had your tonsils out. You are haemorrhaging! You better gargle with saltwater for the next few days and do not eat chops again until your throat heals".

I had a couple of weeks of recuperating. And then I went back to the bank. It was very early, but I was anxious to start work again and as I walked in the back door, a man stooped. He was wearing a big hooded parka and was coming through. I thought it was an intruder and I found a huge stick ready to hit him over the head. When he lifted his head I realised that it was my boss. He had gone fishing very early and was wearing his thick parka with a hood and not his usual suit. We both laughed and he exclaimed, "You're early and anxious to get back to work! And you certainly mean business with that stick!" and we laughed.

It was certainly great to be back at work and enjoy my work and the friendship I had with my workmates. We had lots of work as we were getting ready for the currency changeover. We all worked overtime and often our accountant, Mr Hoffman, who had a sports car, would pile all the staff into it and take us home. There was a lot of hard work and lots of overtime, but we all enjoyed it and had fun.

When I arrived home one afternoon, my brother Eric, *Baba* and *Mama* were all sitting around the kitchen table. They were all looking at me as if I had done something wrong and Eric said to me, "Have you been seeing a man by the name of Nikolaos?"

I looked at all of them and said, "No! I know him from coming to the bank. He had lost a cheque, so I had been serving him. That is all".

Mama said to me, "Well this man has sent a proxy with some friends that Eric knows and he wants to come and see us. He said he knows you. The people he is staying with are Andrew and Souli. Andrew was in hospital when you were there and he had given you some magazines. When Andrew went home he told them that he had seen the young lady who works in the bank, as you were at the hospital at the same time as he was. This man Nikolaos told them that he knew you and would like to marry you. They knew friends of ours, so they came and asked me if it's all right for them to come to ask *Baba* for your hand".

"Well, I don't know him. I only know him from serving him at the bank. That is all." I felt like telling them that I really had a crush on Bill, but I dare not open my mouth as I would be in trouble so I kept quiet.

"They will be coming on the weekend to ask *Baba* for your hand."

"But I don't know him; I only know him from serving him."

The weekend came and the couple who knew my brother brought Nikolaos to our place. They came with a bunch of flowers and they were all smiles. *Baba* sat down and then talked to Nikolaos and asked him what work he did and many other questions. We found out he was an electrician in Greece, but had only arrived a few months ago, and was working as a labourer as he could not speak English to work in his trade. *Baba* asked him why his hands were so soft if he was a tradesman, but he said that at the moment because of not speaking the English language he was not working as an electrician.

I was in the kitchen as I had to get the drinks, a small glass of ouzo for all and *Gliko* (glazed fig) to serve with a glass of cold water to the visitors. My parents came and asked me what I thought of him.

"*Mama*, *Baba*, I do not know him. By only serving him in the bank I cannot tell. Yes he is tall dark and handsome but I don't know the man."

Then *Mama* said, "She loves him. Can't you tell, Gianni? She does love him".

"*Mama*, I don't know, how can I love him? Yes he is tall, dark and handsome, but I don't know what love is."

"Gianni, she loves him," *Mama* repeated.

Baba looked at me and said, "Olympia, do you love him? When I first set eyes on your *Mama* I just knew she was the one for me. Do you love him, Olympia?"

"*Baba*, I just do not know," I said, pleading.

Mama quite firmly said, "of course she loves him. Can't you see? History is repeating itself."

They then went inside and closed the deal and arranged for us to have an engagement the following week, which was end of March. We were to be married on the 22nd of April.

On the following Sunday the engagement ceremony was to take place. But I was working at "Ezi Walking" shoe shop on the Saturday morning and he came and wanted to walk with me to the train station. While we were walking to the train station I told him that I loved working at "Ezi Walking" shoe shop. He stopped and looked at me and said, "You cannot do that when we are married. You cannot handle people's feet. You will have to give that up".

I looked at him in a surprised manner and said "Sorry, what did you say?"

He then repeated himself again. "You must not work there handling people's feet. You will have to give that job away."

I looked at him, very annoyed, and told him, "I think you should go your way and I will go my way. Piss off! Do you hear?" I was fuming. I then walked ahead and got on my train.

When I got home that afternoon *Mama* and Nikolaos were sitting around the kitchen table. I was not very impressed that he was there. *Mama* turned around and said to me, "What will people say? Your engagement is on and the priest is coming tomorrow. You cannot break it up now. What would everyone say?"

"*Mama* can't you see, he cannot tell me what to do. I am not yet married and I love the job. Don't you see?" I said firmly.

"Olympia, Olympia, he did not mean it in a bad way. He cares for you and does not want you to deal with smelly feet. That is all."

Mama was so pleased I was going to be engaged that she did not see that it could be likely that we were not suited for each other. *Mama* was afraid that I would be "left on the shelf" as I was 18 years and 10 months old, past my prime years (as she reasoned).

Sunday came. He had brought a big bunch of flowers and all the family and close friends were there. The priest arrived and blessed the engagement rings, as it was a tradition. That is the first blessing to love and honor each other.

The next day *Mama* said I should go and buy him a watch and give it to him. So at my lunch hour I met him at the Oakleigh Park near the cemetery and gave him a watch. It still puzzles me why I had to do that, possibly to show that I did care for him.

The wedding date was set for the 22nd of April, 1966. *Mama* was all excited and went ahead and planned my wedding.

We visited the place where we hired the wedding dresses and suits. I had my sister and cousins as bridesmaids. The best man and lady-in-waiting were the people he rented the room from at Atkinson St, Oakleigh.

We did not have much money but *Mama* was determined that I should have a big wedding. She invited every relative we had (and all their children) and all her friends and all my workmates. She hired the RSL hall and she decided that we should prepare the food also. There were about 500 people!

She told me to ask my boss for two weeks off, one before the wedding and another week after the wedding. I asked Mr. Rodd, "Is it all right for me to take one week before the wedding and then one after the wedding?"

"He said, "Olympia, why do you need the week before the wedding and then one after?"

I said to him "Mr. Rodd, I have to help *Mama* to cook all the food before the wedding and then we have to clean and tidy after the wedding."

Mr. Rodd shook his head, laughed and said, "Olympia, don't you have a say in this? It is your wedding".

I lifted my shoulders and said, "*Mama* loves to organise everything."

I took the week before and then we cooked chickens, cooked pitas, cut up fetta cheese and made salads, meatballs and cooked meat. We were in the kitchen all week. On Friday we went and set the tables with white tablecloths and set out the entire cutlery that we had hired. Eric had organised the band and the drinks.

Very early in the morning Nikolaos and Tasoula had taken a taxi and had gone to pick up his brother, Gianni, from the airport as he was migrating to Australia. His boat was at Fremantle and so that he could be at the wedding I paid for his plane ticket for him to fly to Melbourne. They waited and waited, but he had missed the plane. I found out that this was because he was gambling on the boat. He had heard the announcement, but he felt that he could not leave his game of cards and so he continued to play. So he never caught the plane from Fremantle to Melbourne as playing cards was more important than anything to him. He did not think it was very important even though they called him a few times over the speakers.

Mama had organised for my sister and me to go to the hairdresser. My hair looked really lovely and they did my entire makeup and they tried to cover a huge cold sore under my nose caused because I was so emotionally hurt. *Baba* went back and forwards taking all the food to the hall. I felt that I had to help him to carry all the food to the RSL hall. We went back and forwards many times as we carried all the food in a wheelbarrow. The wind blew out my hair that the hairdresser had set so nicely.

We had organised for two taxis to pick us all up, but only one turned up so all of us climbed into the taxi, *Mama*, *Baba*, *Giagia*, Tasoula and I, the bride. I just sat in the front seat with the driver while all the rest packed in at the back.

The service was at a house that was to be pulled down eventually so that the church could be built there at Oakleigh. There were lots of people waiting, my workmates and friends and relatives.

We had the reception and my boss gave a speech, as *Baba* was not one for speeches. There was lots of food and dancing, I think all of us were so tired it was hard to enjoy. Nikolaos wanted to go home early, but *Theo* Stellios said. "You are the bridegroom, you can not go home and leave the people behind, it's unheard of". He then slapped Nikolaos for even thinking that. When at last everyone left our family cleaned and tidied the hall.

When we got back home *Mama* had to do the blessing before we came into the house, so Nikolaos and I waited until *Mama* got the icons and the holy water to bless us and then we could go through the door.

There was no honeymoon as Nikolaos had no money and we certainly did not have any as we used all we had for food, the hiring of the RSL hall and for the hiring of the bridal dresses and suits. And, of course, the airplane ticket to bring Gianni from Fremantle to Melbourne!

We lived with my parents, my sister and *Giagia.* Nikolaos' brother, when he eventually arrived in Melbourne, also moved in with us. He was annoyed that we did not wait for him before we got married. I said we had paid your ticket from Fremantle, what happened to you. He said, "I did hear my name called out when I was at Fremantle, but I was really busy as I had a very important game of cards to finish".

#39

As John Wesley said, "The best of all... God is with us."

Nikolaos and I were married for only a month, but we were incompatible. I went to the priest, Father Nikolaos Moutafi, who had married us and said to him, "My parents were strict, but this man is different. We have different likes and dislikes. I would like to end this marriage. He is very different to my people". Father Moutafis said to me, "My child, it takes time to know someone; your parents' marriage was by proxy. They had many ups and downs throughout their life. You must be patient and learn to care for and love each other; it does not happen overnight."

I did persevere with the marriage for 19 years. In 1985, by which time we had moved to Brisbane, I told my husband that definitely we must go our separate ways as we both knew that it was not a happy marriage. I had told him to go away, which he did, but he came back and we lived very turbulent years until 1989 when I packed up and left.

I had to leave quickly as he threatened me. It was an upsetting time for all the family, but that was the road that I chose to take, as he threatened me every time he saw me. My life was not easy. I felt that with Jesus' help all things were possible. Finding my peace was very important than anything else. I knew that God was there to give me hope and a future.

I do feel blessed though as I have two children of whom I am very proud and whom I love dearly. Vasilios and Maria are both married. Vasilios is married to Helen Verbakel and Maria is married to William Richter.

Vasilios and Helen live in Wynnum, a suburb of Brisbane, Queensland. Maria and William live in Perth and have two boys, Zacharia and Samuel.

My niece Olga is married to Michael Latsos and they have two boys, Athanassis and Heraklis. They live in Thessaloniki in Greece. My sister-in-law, Aspasoula, lives with them. I love them all very much but I do not get the opportunity to see them very often. My brother Heraklis was killed in a car accident in 1981 in Greece.

Eric and Anna had the twins, Maria and Debbie and a son, John. Maria is married to Kim Rowe and they have two boys, Harry and Benjamin. They live in Glen Innes in northern NSW. Debbie and her husband, Joe Castellarin, live in Melbourne and have a daughter, Ava. John is married to Regina and also lives in Melbourne.

Eric died with lung cancer on the 16th of October, 2003. During my brother's illness my sister-in-law Anna, had one purpose, taking care of the one she loved. She sat by his side day and night, loving him. Nothing was good enough for him but fresh juices from organically grown vegetables, processed only through a special juicer. His daughter, Maria, who was in Darwin at the time, would send down paw paw leaves for juicing. Debbie was by his side to help, and John searched the web for any kind of food that could help their father. We were all around his bed and Joe, his son-in-law, had brought in a seafood platter as we shared and celebrated his life before he died, which was a couple of days later. Anna, her children, Maria, Debbie, John, my sister Anastasia and I were by his side as he passed away peacefully to a better place where there is no pain, but green gardens and God's love. My sister-in-law, Anna, who I love dearly and am very proud of, is a wonderful sister-in-law, who loves her children and especially dotes on her grandchildren.

Tasoula is married to Kosta Kostas. I love them and I am very close to them. They live in Wheelers Hill, an outer suburb of Melbourne. They have three children, Zafiria, Dimitri and Maria. Zafiria is married to Theo Kafkoulas and they have a son, Ilias and a daughter, Anastasia. Dimitri is married to Claire and they have a daughter, Alexandra. Maria, the youngest, is not married.

Giagia Malamati died on the 11th of November, 1975 in her sleep.

Theo Christopher and *Thea* Ourania had six children, Athanasis (who died in Greece as a baby), Anna (married to John Paioff), Athanasis (who died from a heart attack on 3rd June, 2003), Dianne (married to John La Chance), Kosta (married to Tracey) and Gianni. *Theo* Christopher died from a heart attack on 12th September, 1978. All of these surviving relatives live in Perth.

Anna and John have three children – Kosta, Christopher and Helen.

Kerrie Ann is Dianne's and Mark's daughter.

Kosta's and Tracey's children are Chloe, Christopher and Michael.

Mama had phoned me on the 21st of June for my birthday and she said to me, "Olympia, I saw a dream of a funeral, *Baba* is not well at all, I think it was his funeral I saw, can you come down to Melbourne? "

I said, "*Mama*, I wish I could but I cannot afford the ticket, God be with you both." *Mama* died eight days later, from a heart attack on the 29th of June, 1985. She had actually seen her own funeral, not *Baba's*.

Baba was devastated when he lost *Mama*. Part of him was gone with her and after 54 years of marriage he was lost. *Baba* had Parkinson's disease and suffered for years with it. Unfortunately due to his battle with Parkinson's, *Baba's* personality changed and he was very hard to live with and often very angry. My sister Tasoula and Kon her husband looked after him for two years, but he become very difficult and hard to live with. Then Anna and Eric tried, but eventually he had to be put into a nursing home as he needed high care. He then died with lymphoma on the 25th of January, 1994.

In writing this book I based it on stories told to me by my family, relatives, friends and on my own reflections of my wonderful life.. I tried to find a meaning and to journey within myself. I found that it is one of the hardest journeys one could do, to reflect and grow and move on, to come to terms with how *Mama* had worked hard to help her children and family. She had married at such an early age she never had a chance to enjoy her young life. She did not know any other way. She thought like her parents thought that a girl had to get married and have a husband, children and a home. They did not know that possibly a couple would not be compatible and should get to know each other before taking the step of marriage. *Baba* had no childhood and no youth. All he knew was that he had to work hard, provide for his family and make the best of life. He fought for his country with pride, even though he did not like wars.

Their great faith in God carried them throughout their lives.

Baba's greatest love and joy was his family, and where he met his God was his garden as he saw his plants grow. Australia was the land where he had at last found peace and joy; this was his *Promised Land*.

I found that by reflecting within myself I found peace, strength and joy as I had come to terms with the fact that my parents had tried, under extremely difficult circumstances, their very best to bring us up. They sacrificed so much for their children. I felt with all my trials and tribulations that I was able to grow, to find courage, directions and to know that Jesus was always leading the way, upholding me in my journey. I know that with all my heart that all my family had blessed me in my journey. They helped me that I too can find my God. And I know that Jesus was always leading the way. Knowing that whatever was behind me I must leave behind, but to learn from my mistakes and move on and grow and become a better person. Knowing that only if I forgive and with God's forgiveness and great grace I can move on.

The most wonderful gift I received from my parents was that although they had certainly suffered, they taught me that forgiveness was the only answer to hatred, for one can then move on and live life to the fullest.

I do feel blessed as I am married to a wonderful man now. Tony Pearce and I have the same interests, we love travelling, we love sport and we love reading. Because of our love of traveling we decided to go to St Johann, in the Austrian Tyrol, to be married. Our marriage took place on the 31st of December, 1998, in the snow! We are both retired and live in Brisbane. We have two dogs and two birds, but especially we are blessed with family, children, grandchildren, wonderful friends and peace of mind.

With Tony's encouragement and support I have studied for one year a Ecumenical Hospital Ministry and Pastoral Care course in 2002 at Trinity Theological College, a parttime unit of Clinical Pastoral Education in 2004 at Princess Alexandra Hospital in Brisbane and a full-time Clinical Pastoral Education in 2006 at Greenslopes Hospital in Greenslopes, Brisbane. In 2010 I studied a further unit at Prince Charles Hospital, Chermside and in 2011 another unit at Logan Hospital.

I found it very daunting to go back to school after 40 years. But for me to undertake those studies (and complete them) it was a great challenge and very rewarding. I now work as a volunteer Hospital Chaplain at Logan Hospital and I feel privileged that God has led me along that path.

In October 2008 we went on a trip with Canterbury Tours, "Footsteps of Saint Paul". We visited Turkey, the Greek Islands and Greece. It was a small group, but very personal. The tour guides, Colin and Deidre, were able to organise for my sister, Anastasia, my sister-in-law Anna and my friend Heather and myself to visit my *Baba's* birthplace. When we were in Bursa, Turkey, the guide arranged for us to visit Kouvouklia, my father's village. The homes were still locked since 1922 when my *Baba's* family had fled the village. It was quite an emotional visit. I was so excited and I rang my husband Tony in Australia straight away forgetting that it was 2am in Brisbane. Yelling on the phone "I found my *Baba's* house. It was just incredible". Knowing my heritage, my traditions, my culture, my roots, this is my celebration of freedom and hope in this new land, this is our *Promised Land*. They were all saved by God's great grace through faith.

My parents, brothers, sister and relatives were able to carry each other's burden as quoted in the Bible (Gal 6: 1, 2), building each other up in Christ (Thess 5:11) and encouraging each other to love and serve (Heb 10:24, 25). It was the only way that they were able to survive.

Throughout my life I have always managed to help, support and encourage others with love, and it is by giving that I have received back love and encouragement. That was what I had seen my parents doing in helping and in being there for others. It is God's great grace, which has been with me. Even though I had made many mistakes and had many ups and downs, with all these trials and tribulations I know that I must move on, in order for me to grow and make the best of my life. I cannot look back, but can only move forward and make the best of each day. I too found, like my parents said, by forgiving I can move on and find a purpose in my life. I know that with all my heart God was there for me always as He has blessed me in my life's journey.

Tony and I both thank God every morning for bringing us together and we endeavour to make the best of each day. Knowing that this land is our *Promised Land*.

O Christos Nika Ta Panda

(Christ conquers all)

My First Day at School in Australia
by Olympia Rizidis

It was so strange
So very strange
I could not understand
A word they said
They put me in a class room
I felt so dumb
I cried inside
Oh, It hurt so much
I stared at the blackboard
And tried to understand
A word they said
I sat there mute
And twiddled my thumbs
And thought
Yes I can think
And I can talk
But not in English
But in Greek
Just give me time and I will learn
To read and write again.

My Mama
by Olympia Rizidis

My Mama had missed many things,
As she had married very young
She did not know how to show love
But she had a caring heart
And would lend a hand to anyone
She would listen and help and volunteer us to help
Anyone that was in need
Her love and caring was to teach us
How to cook, sew and clean.
That was her way of showing love
That was her caring heart.
Her door was open to all her friends
To listen, help and care.
That was my Mama.

My Baba
by Olympia Rizidis

My Baba could neither read nor write,
He'd never been to school in all his life.
My Baba was not an educated man,
He'd never been a worldly man,
But life had taught him many things,
He lost his father very young.
He had to work in order to survive.
He'd been to wars, and suffered,
Hardships as a prisoner of war.
But he'd learnt from very young.
To never, never give up.
He'd never seen love in his life
And didn't know how to show love,
He'd only known mother Earth's love,
To dig and fertilise the soil.
He loved his garden,
And lavished love upon his plants,
His garden was his paradise.
He cut the first fruit or a rose
And brought it in with pride,
And gave it to his wife,
To share the miracle of life
It was a simple sign, a simple sign of love.

Giagia, Why Do You Always Wear Black?

by Olympia Rizidis

Giagia, why do you always wear black?
Oh, my little one
We had lands
We had homes
We had loved ones
We had joy and laughter in our hearts.
Oh but on a dark and drizzling day
The evil one came along
Spreading fear and terror in our hearts
We were kicked out of our homes
And sent to strange lands
Some of us survived
To tell our tale
But many died in refugee camps
And were buried in mass graves
Lost forever
Parents, husbands, wives, daughters and sons.
Lost in the war
Oh yes I wear black
For I grieve for my lost child.

About the Author

Olympia Rizidis was born in June 1947 in Florina, Northern Greece during the civil war, and spent her early childhood in Greece. In 1955 she migrated to Australia with her family. She loves it here as she did not have to work in the fields but could attend school. She went to school in Victoria until grade 10. She then worked in a bank; got married and raised a son and a daughter. She moved to Queensland in 1976 and studied chaplaincy and 4 units in Clinical Pastoral Education. She is a volunteer chaplain and enjoys reading and writing.

She was inspired by Susanna De Vries' book *Blue Ribbons, Bitter Bread* as that book touched on the horrendous ordeals that her family went through, in the exchange of the populace of Greece and Turkey. Olympia had heard many stories told by her grandmother and her parents, so she started a long journey of researching from immigration and marine museums records to Googling. She visited Turkey and Greece. In Turkey she found her father's house still locked up as they had left it in 1922. She also interviewed relatives and friends both in Greece and in Australia to write this book.